Untangling
Your Marriage

All my Best,
Danci

Untangling Your Marriage

A Guide to Collaborative Divorce

Nanci A. Smith

ROWMAN & LITTLEFIELD
Lanham • Boulder • New York • London

Published by Rowman & Littlefield
An imprint of The Rowman & Littlefield Publishing Group, Inc.
4501 Forbes Boulevard, Suite 200, Lanham, Maryland 20706
www.rowman.com

86-90 Paul Street, London EC2A 4NE

British Library Cataloguing in Publication Information Available

Library of Congress Cataloging-in-Publication Data

Names: Smith, Nanci A., 1966– author.
Title: Untangling your marriage : a guide to collaborative divorce / Nanci
  A. Smith, JD.
Description: Lanham, Maryland : Rowman & Littlefield, [2022] | Includes
  bibliographical references and index. | Summary: "More than 800,000
  people each year in the United State get divorced. This book invites the
  reader into a more meaningful conversation about how to end a marriage
  with dignity and mutual respect, using the interdisciplinary model
  called Collaborative Divorce"— Provided by publisher.
Identifiers: LCCN 2022004604 (print) | LCCN 2022004605 (ebook) | ISBN
  9781538166895 (cloth) | ISBN 9781538166901 (ebook)
Subjects: LCSH: Divorce—United States. | Collaborative divorce—United
  States. | Marriage—United States.
Classification: LCC HQ834 .S64 2022 (print) | LCC HQ834 (ebook) | DDC
  306.890973—dc23/eng/20220207
LC record available at https://lccn.loc.gov/2022004604
LC ebook record available at https://lccn.loc.gov/2022004605

For Natalie and Gregg:
without you both, this book would not be possible.

Contents

PART III: YOUR EMERGENT FUTURE IS NOW

Acknowledgments

It is with deep gratitude that I wish to acknowledge the many people who have made it possible for me to find the courage to share my perspectives on divorce. It will not be possible to name you all, but to my clients over the course of my career, I extend my most sincere appreciation for trusting me with your most intimate and vulnerable selves. I hope this work does you proud.

To my parents, Sandy and Rhoda Smith, words cannot express my love and appreciation for your unwavering support. Sixty years of marriage is quite a blessing and an example of how it can be done.

To my development editor, Paula Diaco, your early and consistent enthusiasm, keen eye, and laughter sustained me when I doubted that this book would ever come into existence.

To my literary agent, Katharine Sands, thank you for your patience, wisdom, and belief in this project finding a home.

To Suzanne Staszak-Silva and the team at Rowman & Littlefield, thank you for believing in me and the collaborative divorce model.

To the greater collaborative divorce community, it has been my absolute delight to know that you exist. You are the fresh air in an otherwise stagnant room. From Stu Webb starting this movement, to early adopters Pauline Tesler and Woody Mosten; to next gen adapters Jacinta Gallant, Victoria Smith, Deborah Gilman, George Richardson, Ed Sachs and Eric Sachs at My Collaborative Teams. To Carol Hughes for helping us remember the impact of divorce on adult children; and to all collaborative colleagues across the country who have never wavered in their commitment to shifting the paradigm of divorce to improve the lives of divorcing couples and their families. I am proud to be a part of your community.

To my local collaborative practice group, CPVT, I am so grateful to have you to practice, grow, and learn from. Thank you from the bottom of my heart for your willingness to stay together as we steadfastly grew our skills and our experiences even when we didn't have any clients. Thank you, E. Darby Herrington, Richard Witte, Lindsey Huddle, Kate Suskin, Corey Wood, Kate Vandenbergh, Michelle Tarnelli, Marcy Milton, Theo Kennedy, Kurt Hughes, Brittany LeBerge, Scott Ward, Lori Lustberg, and Michelle Cortez-Hawkins. Special thanks are due to Cathy Daigle, whose multi-decade commitment to collaborative practice in California, Vermont, and at the IACP has been inspiring to witness.

To my former mentor and colleague Kimberly B. Cheney, thank you for the support and grace you showed me as a young attorney and for bringing me up right; to Alan Biederman, for introducing me to the spirit of a trial attorney and insisting on nothing short of excellence in the preparation for and the execution of an adversarial trial. To Bunny and Peter Flint for your early mentorship and enduring friendship.

Special thanks are due to Lucia White for helping me keep the shop running smoothly, for your commitment to mediation, and your unwavering empathy to our clients. I am so excited that you are here as we transition the firm into a fully non-adversarial mediation and collaborative divorce practice.

To my friend and colleague Susan Palmer, thank you for introducing me to the world of systems theory, organizational development, executive leadership coaching, and for turning me on to some of the world's most innovative and extraordinary system change thinkers, poets, and leaders. Your curiosity, enthusiasm for personal growth, and friendship have sustained me through the dark years after my own divorce. It was through my learnings with you that I have found my voice and my willingness to step into a leadership role to share what I currently know about divorce and to bring collaborative divorce into the mainstream.

Thank you to all the teachers, coaches, friends, colleagues, and loved ones who have passed through my life and enriched it. I would not be here if it were not for you.

And finally, a deep bow of gratitude and appreciation to anyone who is reading this. It is my sincerest hope that you find this useful and that it gives you courage to divorce differently.

I take full responsibility for the content of this book. The thoughts are my own, and credit is given when due. Any errors or omissions are entirely my own.

Vermont, December 2021
Nanci A. Smith, Esq.

Introduction

COMPLEXITY, GROWTH, AND COLLABORATIVE DIVORCE: LET'S GET STARTED

On a macro level, we are living in a time of volatility, uncertainty, complexity, and ambiguity (VUCA). This was a phrase the U.S. military used to describe the post-Cold War era, which has since been adopted by current thought leaders in organizational development and executive leadership circles.

On a micro level, the period of going through divorce is exactly like that. The most effective strategies in times of VUCA are to remain open for possibilities, to innovate, to remain nimble, to set safe boundaries that are not too rigid, and to allow enough room to experiment. When it comes to your divorce, you (and your spouse, if he or she chooses to come along for the ride) are being asked to become the leader of your newly evolving family. This is an opportunity for personal growth and transformational change.

You are being given an opportunity to create the next iteration of yourself; a new parenting paradigm and a new relationship with your spouse and extended family and friends. The times are changing, and you can exert more control over your divorce process than you may realize. Collaborative divorce, an out-of-court dispute resolution model, fits this paradigm of thinking and is a way to make meaning of your life during your divorce.

There are only four ways to get divorced:

1. do-it-yourself;
2. use a mediator, with or without lawyers;

3. go to court, with or without lawyers, and conform to an adversarial process; or
4. choose a collaborative divorce process.

Divorce represents massive change and disruption to the status quo. You must contend with the day-to-day grief that gnaws (or pounds) your heart and head while you keep working, shopping, maintaining the house, animals, children, elderly parents, bosses, friends, and family. With so much being asked of you, you may think you don't have time to focus on your own physical, mental, and emotional well-being. It is common to feel as if your life is falling apart, and you simply don't have the energy to create a new paradigm. It may be easier to just feel mad, or sad, point the blame at your spouse for ruining your life, and turn it all over to a divorce lawyer.

This book is intended to assure you that your psycho-spiritual-emotional health is the key to a successful legal divorce. My intention in this book is to provide you with the basics for how to do that by introducing you to collaborative divorce, a relatively new divorce process that is fully legal, radically supportive, and downright practical. Collaborative divorce is both a process and a mind-set. It is practiced in every state in the United States. It is also practiced throughout the world, in Canada, Australia, Italy, England, and Israel, among other countries.

WHAT IS COLLABORATIVE DIVORCE?

About thirty years ago in Minnesota, two veteran family lawyers, Stuart Webb and his colleague and friend Ron Ousky, decided that they had had enough of tearing families apart through an adversarial process just so the couple could live in separate homes, set up a parenting schedule, and come to an allocation of financial resources so that both spouses could live a decent life.

They decided to try something different. Each agreed that they would only settle cases through direct negotiations, with each other and the clients. They agreed not to go to court anymore. They dubbed the phrase collaborative divorce; they settled cases without the need to face off in court, they felt good about themselves, and their clients appreciated their efforts.

The idea resonated with other lawyers, so Webb and Ousky wrote a book.[1] Next, a no-nonsense, innovative lawyer named Pauline Tesler took the idea a step further when she and her mental health colleagues thought the model could benefit from integrating mental health professionals and financial neutrals. In this model, no longer were just lawyers at the negotiating table trying to do the work of three separate professionals: legal, mental health, and financial.[2] Now, skillful and interdisciplinary professionals were available to form a team to assist the clients through all three aspects of every divorce: the emotional, the financial, and the legal. The marital dynamic in collaborative divorce was explained in a way that mental health professionals who were interested in being team members and their collaborative attorney counterparts could start to break down and understand why divorce negotiations can be so challenging.[3] Standards of practice were created by the International Academy of Collaborative Professionals (IACP), and best practices, trainings, and networking for like-minded professionals took off.[4]

Collaborative divorce has grown and evolved over time through the courage and convictions of a generation of lawyers who were willing to challenge the dominant, adversarial, and litigious divorce paradigm. Because of the efforts of these collaborative professionals across the country and the world, collaborative divorce is now recognized by the American Bar Association and state courts as a form of dispute resolution.

The Uniform Law Commissions has helped create legislation across the country so that the public understands this as a form of limited representation by lawyers for an out-of-court dispute resolution process.[5] It's known as a form of "limited representation" or "unbundled legal services," because you hire a lawyer for settlement purposes only. When you hire a lawyer to represent you in a collaborative divorce, she will not go to court to engage in an adversarial battle on your behalf. Period. If you (or your spouse) choose to end the process, then you will need to retain new litigation counsel. This is known as the "disqualification clause," which is contained in the participation agreement. As the client, the participation agreement is your informed consent. It sets the tone for your divorce, and in it you will see what you gain from this process and what types of adversarial tactics you will be giving up in exchange. A sample participation agreement can be found in the appendix.

Collaborative divorce is defined by the existence of a participation agreement and the disqualification clause—participants are bound by the agreement to proceed in this manner. If that bothers you, then collaborative divorce may not be the best process for you. You can still consider mediation or litigation. This book is your guide to successfully completing the collaborative divorce process using an interdisciplinary team approach as it is commonly practiced across the country.

When you choose to engage in a collaborative divorce process, we all expect that you will treat yourself, your spouse, and the members of your team with dignity and mutual respect. You can rest assured that no one is trying to take advantage of you. You will have time and space to gather your thoughts and ask questions. The team is invested in your success. We help you identify why you are here and what you hope to achieve by doing your divorce differently; we provide a place to discuss your hopes for your future relationships and financial security, and your concerns and fears; we help you collect and organize the relevant information that we need to help you generate thoughtful, practical, and durable resolutions. We assess the viability of your options; you make decisions on your time line, not that of the court, that works for both of you and your family. A visual representation of the process can be found in the appendix.[6]

We use some tools to keep us all on track. We help you identify goals: short-term, medium, and long-term. We create a "road map," which is an outline of what to expect from your divorce process, so you always know where you are in the process. A sample road map is in the appendix. We meet as a full team when we have something important to talk about. Otherwise, we support you talking with either the coach or the financial neutral, depending on which issues are "up" for you, either jointly or separately. We understand that no two people experience the process in the same way. Your needs and the needs of your spouse may align on some things and differ in other respects. There is room to meet both of your needs.

How long this process takes depends on whether you and your spouse are both "psychologically ready" to be divorced. Most couples can complete their collaborative divorce in between six months and year. It can be more or less, depending on your needs. We talk about this early in the process. What is your preferred time line? Does your spouse agree? This process is designed for efficiency. It is generally less expensive than litigation. The cost of any divorce is directly related to the level of conflict and your willingness to work through the emotional issues before you tackle the legal and financial issues. More conflict and the lack of readiness to move on increase costs. If you wanted the divorce done yesterday, but your spouse just found out you want a divorce, you will be counseled to slow down and let your spouse catch up. The spouse on the receiving end is usually shocked at first but can quickly adapt to the new reality with the correct support. This requires using empathy.

The end goal of the process is a divorce agreement that is sustainable and about which you feel OK. The agreement will be drafted by the lawyers and filed with the court. You will likely receive your divorce decree in the mail. In many states, you never have to step foot in a courthouse, and you have the satisfaction that you handled your divorce with dignity and discretion. You will likely feel proud of yourselves. You have an excellent chance of being friends and good co-parents to your children; you have the opportunity to heal from the shock of a divorce, and you can choose to maintain a sense of family, even if you are now living in separate houses.

DIVORCE IS LEGAL, EMOTIONAL, AND FINANCIAL—
THAT'S WHY WE HAVE A TEAM

Divorce and separation affect people on many different levels—legal, financial, emotional, spiritual, physical, and psychological. Let's meet the team.

The Collaborative Divorce Lawyer

Each spouse has a collaborative divorce lawyer who has received advanced training in non-adversarial negotiation techniques and is part of the team. The ethical rules for lawyers prohibit one lawyer from representing two people with potentially conflicting interests, so no, you can't just have one lawyer working for both of you, even if you get along. A side note: A mediator is a single person who helps you and your spouse reach an agreement. Mediators may be lawyers, but they cannot give legal advice to you or your spouse while serving as a mediator.

A good mediator will always encourage you to have your mediation agreement reviewed by an independent family lawyer before you sign off. The lawyers in a collaborative divorce are neither the "leaders" nor the dominant voices in the group. The lawyers should act as members of a fully functioning team of professionals. Your lawyer will advocate for you without being a bully. Your lawyer makes sure that your interests are identified and heard. In addition, your lawyer provides you legal counsel throughout the process and is there to be helpful, not to make a difficult situation worse. The lawyer is there to answer all your questions about how to dissolve your marriage, legally. Your lawyer is your advocate, your guide and adviser. Your lawyer will analyze the data and help you generate ideas, make informed decisions, and draft agreements.

The lawyers draft all the paperwork necessary for an uncontested divorce, including the required court forms. The lawyers file the paperwork. Depending on your local court rules, you either will be divorced by the court sending your divorce decree by the mail, or you may be required to make a short appearance in court or via video for an uncontested hearing, and then your divorce will be granted. If that happens, your lawyers will be with you and can explain what to expect.

The Neutral Mental Health Coach

In some states each spouse has a different neutral mental health coach. In other places, a single coach is part of the team. So, you may hear about a "one-coach model" or a "two-coach model," depending on your location. Mental health professionals are highly skilled in helping people through the emotional divorce process, which is often experienced as a grieving process. They understand family systems and dynamics.

They are here to help you manage your intense emotions so you can respond appropriately. They help you communicate more effectively, and perhaps for the first time in your marriage, you learn to present yourself confidently in a way that you are understood and feel heard. You can develop a common narrative for how to speak to your children, or your extended family or community. Coaches are not here to provide couples therapy, or make clinical diagnoses (that is for your own private therapist or psychiatrist); they are here to help you identify and articulate your goals and interests.

They are excellent resources when you have questions about the impact of divorce on your children: for example, how to co-parent effectively whether your kids are minors, young adults, or older children with their own families. They are here to normalize the intense emotions you probably are feeling. Once the collaborative case is completed, the mental health neutrals cannot serve as a therapist for anyone in the family. This preserves their neutrality.

The Financial Neutral

Financial neutrals are specially trained to understand and analyze your family's financial reality. As neutral, unbiased financial professionals, they facilitate difficult conversations about money, which is often a sensitive topic in divorce. Financial neutrals help focus attention on short-term immediate financial concerns as well as the longer view toward retirement.

Their role is to identify financial needs and understand the total financial picture; they analyze financial data so that you can have accurate information about income, assets, liabilities, and cash flow. They create budgets and understand that children have special costs and needs that also must be considered. They help you generate different settlement options so that you can understand the short- and long-term impact of decisions made during the divorce.

Financial neutrals are also skilled at facilitating communication and can help educate the spouse who may have deferred financial decision making to the other spouse throughout the marriage. This is a common dynamic in many marriages. The financial neutral is here to provide creative and helpful solutions to often complex financial challenges. Financial neutrals will not sell you products or otherwise attempt to manage your money in the future. That role is for your own financial planner or broker.

Child Specialist

Whether your children are minors or adults, a child specialist can provide guidance by bringing the voice of the children into the process, as they are sure to have opinions. The child specialist is a mental health professional with specialized interest and knowledge about children whose parents are separating and divorcing. Sometimes the neutral mental health coach can serve in this role, but sometimes a separate professional who is solely focused on the children is a good idea. This professional will help you understand the developmental needs of each child and how to help them adjust to the divorce. They provide a private place for the children to voice their concerns or express their opinions about living preferences or parenting issues; they provide a perspective and information, from the child's point of view, to help you make more informed decisions about co-parenting; and they are excellent at conflict management in the event that there are strong and different feelings about parenting. They talk with the children and you about divorce and the impact on children. The child specialist can provide unique insights into the children's experience of divorce and can help guide decisions about parenting plans and sharing time between two homes.

PUTTING IT ALL TOGETHER

The team members meet as often as necessary to keep the divorce process moving forward, but at a pace that makes sense for the family as a whole. You meet with the correct professional at the time you need him most. For example, you may meet with the coach to talk about ways to tell the children and family; ways to improve communication as the divorce process continues to unfold, and you can talk about parenting plans, or emotional hot spots or triggers as they occur, so that you do not build up resentments toward your spouse.

When you have provided the financial neutral with all the requested data, you will likely meet together to assess the data and understand it. Sometimes the lawyers are present, sometimes it is just the client and the neutral. The lawyers only show up when we have to or when it is helpful, mindful that our hourly rate is often the highest. We allow our colleagues to do their work. We are still available to you if you have questions, or when you need support, but the process is more efficient the more we allow the correct professionals to do their jobs at the right time in the process.

When it is time to come together as a full team (both lawyers, the coach, and the financial neutral), we have an agenda that was planned in advance with your input. We meet because there is a purpose: something needs to be done. Perhaps we are discussing goals, or we are reviewing important financial information, or we are discussing ideas for final settlement. Each of us does our homework between meetings to keep the process moving along. The team members may meet without you. This is to make sure that we are all on the same page and we are accountable to each other. The end result of a collaborative divorce is a fully "uncontested" divorce.

If you are interested, the team can even help you put together a goodbye ritual to honor the marriage and the hard work of the divorce. This is the final step so that you can have some emotional closure on this important chapter of your life. Because your final divorce decree is likely to come in the mail, on a piece of paper, without any bells or whistles, it is rather anticlimactic; and doing something to end the marriage makes sense, even if it is just coming together one last time as a team, to honor the hard work and effort you made to get to this point.

This does not mean that the work of getting divorced in a collaborative process is easy. Nothing about getting divorced is easy. It is a matter of degrees.

LET'S TALK LOGISTICS

You think this sounds intriguing, and you might be interested. How and when do you tell your spouse? How do you know if you are a good candidate for this process? What can you expect? How do you find the right lawyer? This book is designed to answer all of those questions and more. It is also important to remember that every case is different, and depending on where you live, collaborative divorce might be practiced a little differently, so you need to be able to go with the flow.

What is always true about a collaborative divorce case, regardless of where you live, is the participation agreement and the disqualification clause for the lawyers. A sample participation agreement is included in the appendix.

Once you sign the participation agreement, your lawyers will not go to court with you. If you don't sign a participation agreement with the disqualification clause, you are not engaged in a collaborative divorce process as defined by the International Academy of Collaborative Professionals. You could be in some other kind of process, sometimes referred to as a "cooperative" divorce, but it is not a true collaborative divorce.

The IACP sets the gold standard to which most experienced collaborative professionals hold ourselves as it has the most rigorous training requirements, the highest ethical standards, and some of the smartest, kindest professionals you will ever want to meet, even under the difficult circumstances of a divorce. These are the people you want on your team.

ARE SOME PEOPLE NOT SUITED TO THIS PROCESS?

Yes, just like some lawyers will not interested or well-suited to practice collaborative divorce, some couples will not be well-suited to this type of dispute resolution process. This is why it is essential that you interview a collaborative lawyer and share the particulars of your situation with counsel to guide you toward the most effective process for you. This is also why we have you both talk with an experienced mental health professional before we start a collaborative divorce process.

We need to make sure that neither you nor your spouse have any latent mental health or other issues that would interfere with the process. The professionals want a successful outcome for you, and we don't want to start a case that we don't think we can finish together.

No hard and fast rules make you eligible for a collaborative divorce, except that you both need to be able to communicate with each other directly and follow through on basic assignments and agreements. It is important to screen yourselves honestly to ensure that this process will work for you. If you are a victim of domestic violence or if there is active, untreated addiction or other mental health issues, you want to be up front about those issues so the team can honestly assess whether we all agree that this process will be safe and effective. Serious mental health issues or prior domestic violence does not automatically disqualify a couple.

If a serious personality disorder in one spouse will make reaching a negotiated resolution impossible, then collaborative divorce will not generally be an appropriate option. Otherwise, no matter how difficult your circumstances, a collaborative divorce should be an option to consider, because going to court often makes a difficult situation worse by setting up a public, adversarial battle of very private, challenging personal issues.

A LITTLE INSIGHT INTO THE MIND OF A DIVORCE LAWYER

Before you do anything else (including telling your spouse that you want to divorce) consider the fact that if you call a divorce lawyer trained in the dark art of adversarial warfare, the risk is very real that things will go from bad to worse in a hurry. It also will cost a small fortune in attorney's fees, and the interests of your children will likely get lost amid the turmoil.

This is not because you or your spouse are bad or evil people (although sometimes it is), or that your spouse's lawyer is a jerk (although sometimes he is). Rather, *it is in the nature of the adversarial divorce process and its failure to account for the grief* you and everyone in your family and circle of friends are experiencing. In a traditional divorce model, we don't acknowledge the grief involved in a divorce. We didn't have healthy rituals to end a marriage or long-term relationship with dignity and mutual respect until collaborative divorce came along. Now we do.

Our culture values the wedding industry, regardless of the fact that half of all marriages end in divorce. The failure of society to embrace a collaborative divorce model, one of compassion, dignity, and mutual respect, is a disservice to all of us. That is why I wrote this book: for you; so, you can change the paradigm by asking for what you want from your divorce lawyer and from the current divorce operating system; so, you can recommend the process to others; so, the sting in divorce can be diminished.

Grief, coupled with a process that makes you and your spouse adversaries, creates an environment where good people behave badly and everyone suffers, except the lawyers. We do our job, get paid, and walk away from your often broken and hostile reality, leaving you to deal with that mess on your own. Collaborative divorce offers an alternative approach, but it requires that you, the client, set the tone and expectations.

I know you may not feel you have the capacity to stand up to your lawyer at this point in your process, but I'm here to encourage you to stand up for yourself and your family (including your spouse) even though it feels uncomfortable and challenging. Be brave. Find the courage to say that you want an amicable, non-adversarial divorce where you and your spouse can emerge healthy and wholehearted, not bitter and resentful.

Divorce lawyers sometimes contribute to the negativity. This is not because we are mean spirited or just greedy (although some of us are, as in any profession). We are trained to "take our clients as we find them," solve problems, and be "zealous advocates" for you. We follow your instructions at a time when your heart feels broken, and you are filled with anxiety and fear.

You may not be thinking straight when feelings such as betrayal, shame, guilt, or rage are driving you to the divorce lawyer for your first consultation to get oriented as to what to expect. Lawyers are not mental health professionals. We tend to use that as an excuse not to deal with your emotions or the emotional impact your divorce is having on you or your family. We think it's not our job. We aren't trained for that, and we prefer to quickly refer you to a qualified mental health professional to deal with that aspect of your divorce, while we prepare the papers to file for divorce.

WHAT IS THE DEAL WITH COLLABORATIVE DIVORCE LAWYERS, AND WHY ARE THEY DIFFERENT?

Collaborative divorce lawyers are different from traditional divorce lawyers. We have not forgotten that another word for lawyer is "counselor at law." I'm not suggesting that lawyers should act like mental health professionals. I'm just saying that we could do a better job of acknowledging the intense emotions and the grieving process that divorce presents. It doesn't take a PhD in psychology to demonstrate a little more empathy and compassion for a suffering human being.

Collaborative divorce lawyers agree not to make a difficult situation worse. We can handle your strong emotions with sensitivity and understanding. We don't let your feelings get in the way of progress, and we help you set reasonable expectations to move forward at a pace that works—we don't stonewall, and we don't rush. The professional team model not only helps you and your spouse, it also helps your lawyer not default to our original training and adversarial ways.

This is important, because for attorneys trained in traditional adversarial practices, it is not easy to shift our paradigm, approach, or attitudes, even if we want to. The old approach served most of us well for a large part of our careers, and there is always resistance to change, even when we know it is good for us.

Getting divorced is a scary time of life. Few among us have seen a healthy divorce model, and most people experience divorce as a catastrophic life experience; it is considered an adverse risk for minor children, and the impact on adult children can be significant as well. Going to court sounds awful, but people think that it is the only way. This is not true anymore.

Without understanding that there is a different and appropriate path to follow, you may think you want us to be your knight, gladiator, pit bull, shark, or whatever image conveys the toughest lawyer in town. In that paradigm, and with that attitude, we all lose some of our common humanity.

Within the adversarial system's limits, divorce lawyers do not generally see ourselves as healers or peacemakers. We often buy into the stereotypes that society places upon us through popular culture, and we create an endless self-fulfilling prophecy. As the client, you have the power to change this cycle with your divorce.

I remember one time early in my career as a trial lawyer, I was assigned by the court to represent children in a hostile divorce and custody case. During the hearing, the wife was not happy that I was involved in the case. She spat at me in court one day that I was a "barracuda" trying to take her children from her. To be honest, at that time, I did not consider that an insult.

To a young lawyer or to one not trained in the interdisciplinary collaborative divorce process, your grief may appear in our office as anger. You seem really upset. You may be crying. You may be focused on every rotten thing your spouse has done to you. You may instruct us to "go for the jugular" because at the time you first meet us, you are afraid and deeply wounded. You may want to strike out and fight back, or surrender completely because of a sense of overwhelming guilt or shame. Your reptilian brain is in overdrive. Your amygdala has been hijacked. You are fight or flight personified. You are stressed out, on high alert, and you appear to us very credible and sympathetic. We want to help you stand up for yourself and protect you.

Traditional divorce lawyers are trained to fight with words and trial advocacy skills. We do this within very broad canons of ethical rules. We follow your instructions and try to achieve the goals you tell us you want. Unfortunately, the lawyers sometimes don't realize that your goals may change a few months down the road as your grief moves into a new stage.

I'm suggesting that you slow down a bit. Take time to consider your options. Explore your core values and align them to serve your best interests and the best interests of your family as a whole, despite your pain and grief.

You are the most important role model for your children. This is true, regardless of how your ex deals with his or her experience of the divorce process. How they handle themselves is not your responsibility. Their behavior is not a reflection on you. The sooner you accept that you are not in control over your spouse, the easier your divorce will be for the family. This is true in a traditional divorce or a collaborative one.

How you think and behave during your divorce process is your responsibility and within your control. Be brave. Trust yourself. You can handle what is going on. Use this experience to make you stronger. Do not let it deplete you. Finding the right attorney, mental health coach, and financial neutral are essential ingredients to emerging from this process better than you started it. We are all here under the umbrella of the collaborative divorce process, waiting to serve.

Thoughts to Consider

If you are the initiating spouse: How and when will I speak with my spouse? What will I say? Do I know what I am talking about? How will I respond to my spouse's reaction?

Thoughts to Consider

If you are the receiving spouse: How will I process this information? Who are my sources of emotional support? Are they the most appropriate at this time? How do I want to behave? What are my core values? How can my actions be consistent with my values?

Thoughts to Let Go

I hate my spouse. My spouse caused this mess. I'll never forgive. I'll never recover from the shame and embarrassment. I will be ruined financially. Our children will be ruined. I can't handle this.

Practical Tips

Read up on how to have a difficult conversation.[7] Speak your truth, then stop talking. Don't justify, defend, or convince. Find skillful mental health professionals for you both to process this change. Your spouse is no longer your emotional go-to person.

If you receive the news, take time and say, "OK. Thanks for sharing that. I need some time to process this."

Build your support network. Use your collaborative divorce lawyer and your new therapist as the process is about to start.

Part I

THE BASIC STRUCTURE OF A DIVORCE

To Break a Promise

Make a place of prayer, no fuss now,
just lean into the white brilliance
and say what you needed to say
all along, nothing too much, words
as simple as yours and as heard
as the birdsong above your head
or the river running gently beside you.

Let your words join one to another
the way stone nestles on stone,
the way water just leaves
and goes to the sea,
the way your promise
breathes and belongs
with every other promise
the world has ever made.

Now, let them go on,
leave your words
to carry their own life
without you, let the promise
go with the river.
Stand up now. Have faith. Walk away.

—David Whyte[1]

1

Facing Reality Is Not Fun, But It Is Necessary

This is a hard and confusing time. It may be months or years in the making. You may have felt something brewing, but you did not want to address it head-on for fear that it would lead to a divorce. Divorce is the last thing in the world any couple wants. Maybe you decided to try marriage counseling. At some point, someone usually walks out in a huff, feeling misunderstood again, and the dynamic continues until someone calls it quits.

As a younger divorce lawyer, I would often think that by the time a couple reached out for marriage counseling, it was already too late, so why bother? Now I believe that if you haven't found a good marital counselor, you really should give it an earnest effort before saying the "D" word. Regardless of the issues in your marriage, any effort to sit down and use your words in a safe environment is worth the effort before you start a divorce process. A therapeutic paradigm called discernment therapy is a time-limited, focused process used by a professional certified in this method to assess the ambivalence factor that is usually present in one or both of you when the topic of divorce is explored.

I submit that spending at least four to eight sessions with a skillful therapist that you both find to be reasonable and supportive is a good step forward, even if it becomes clear that divorce is the best solution for one or both of you. Sometimes, the marriage has just gone too far in the wrong direction, and contempt and disrespect have set in. If that is where you are, I won't lie. That is a big and likely insurmountable hurdle to overcome if you plan to save a marriage.

If you've tried and you are ready to divorce, then it is time to admit the obvious and declare that the marriage is no longer working. That does not mean you start calling divorce lawyers who pride themselves on their litigation skills. You need sound advice, not hyperbole. You need to learn how to break up with dignity so that you do not destroy yourself and your children while you pursue a holy war against your ex. I'm just saying, litigious divorces don't work out the way people fantasize they will.

LACK OF COMMUNICATION—
WHY THERAPY IS SO IMPORTANT

You may be curious about the reasons people say they are getting divorced. It boils down to a fundamental lack of honest communication. It doesn't matter if the communication problem manifests over money, sex, power and control, listening, infidelity, addiction, or snoring. All of those problems can be worked through if you are able to communicate your feelings. Many of us are not well trained in discussing our feelings—alas, another good reason to enlist the help of a skilled mental health professional at the outset of the divorce process.

The third or fourth question I ask in any initial interview with a potential new client is if they have a therapist. For the client who answers in the affirmative, it shows me that he or she has insight and at least understands that a therapist will be useful during a divorce. For the others, the conversation goes something like this:

Nanci (head cocking to the side, but looking the client straight in the eye): "So, who is your therapist?"

Client (super-defensively): "Why? I don't have one. I'm not the one with the problem. It's my spouse who has all the problems."

Nanci (thinking to herself: *Oh, boy.*): "No worries. I'll give you a list of potential people before you leave."

Client: "I don't understand. Didn't you hear me? I'm fine. Really. Why do you think I need a therapist?"

Nanci: "All of my clients have a therapist. You just do. Divorce is complex. You will feel a lot of things, and although you may want to just call and talk with me, I'm too expensive, and I'm not qualified to deal with that stuff. Plus, you have to have one if you want me to be your lawyer."

The air is either sucked out of the room, the interview is over, and the client visibly offended exits, stage left, or we continue to talk about where the client is and explore options. I rarely sign a client on the first meeting: I give clients space to process this very big decision.

ADMITTING THAT YOU ARE NOT HAPPY

At some point in your marriage, you or your spouse started to notice how unhappy you are; either an unhealthy silence has settled in, or the fighting has become out of control. It doesn't matter. It has the same effect. You admit to yourself, at least, that you are not happy.

I remember driving home on my forty-minute commute from the office fantasizing about a small, white condo where I was certain I would be happier than my lovely house in the country. In my mind, I would have no one to answer to when I got home, no pressure to do or be something that I was not feeling, and I would not have to deal with the disappointment that the conversation I wanted to have would not happen.

On my ride, I'd push away the vision of the condo, and I'd think, *No. Tonight, I'm going to try hard to . . .*

Fill in the blank: be nice, have sex, do the dishes, make a nice meal, talk about my feelings. It just never happened that way. The truth was that I just didn't want to go home anymore because I knew it would end in a fight I could not win, and I'd feel frustrated and alone.

Nothing is worse than feeling alone when you are in a relationship. I'd rather be alone and lonely than be in a marriage feeling lonely. But that's just me. I digress, but I see this often in my clients and want to prepare you for what may be ahead. That, and the fact that you are reading this book leads me to believe that you have reached a place of no return. Let's turn this conversation back to you, then.

Express yourself. Use your words. Start by acknowledging the need to have a difficult conversation. The adage "Say what you mean, mean what you say, and don't say it mean" is a good motto to live by during a divorce, and beyond.

Now you have done it. You and your spouse have had the discussion that one or both of you are not happy, and someone mentioned the "D" word. Try to make sure the children are asleep and not overhearing this one. It is not for them to know or worry about until you, as the adults, have a plan. This may take some time and thought. As hard as it may be, try to put together a plan of action that would work for your family as a whole. Resist the temptation to call the meanest divorce lawyer you know tomorrow. Do not file for divorce right now. You have time.

I urge you to discuss with your spouse how you can get through this process without destroying each other and your family. You will both want and need to consult or retain a divorce lawyer when you are ready to put it all in writing, but you are nowhere near that point in your process. For goodness' sake, it's just been a day or two.

TIME TO CONSULT A MENTAL HEALTH PROFESSIONAL AS A COACH

Address the emotional impact of the divorce first before you try to tackle the legal and financial aspects, or other logistics, of which there are plenty. It is easy to become overwhelmed with fear and anxiety about a future you cannot see or control. That is why you start first by preparing yourselves for the emotional or psychological divorce.

Remember how I said that if you are trying to save your marriage, marriage counseling probably won't work? That is true, but this is different. The point of consulting and working with the mental health professional now is not to save your marriage, but to save your friendship and ability to co-parent if you have children.

Do you see the difference here? You don't have to stay in an unhealthy or unhappy marriage, but you do have to stay cordial so that you can co-parent your children and not destroy yourselves and your children through a bitter divorce.

If you take the time, however much you both need so that you are both psychologically ready to be divorced, you will be in a much better frame of mind to work with an attorney. You will save thousands of dollars in attorney's fees when you are not consumed by negative emotions and using your lawyer and the adversarial system to play out your angry, one-sided narrative.

Here are some important questions and concepts you should consider and talk with each other about in a co-parenting coaching session:

How do I feel today? It is OK to feel sad, mad, frustrated, confused, angry, betrayed, annoyed, anxious, afraid, rageful, depressed, relieved, hopeful, or excited.

A lot of emotions are swirling around, especially in the early stages. You want to ask yourself, *How will we tell the children, family, friends, and community? Can we create a common narrative that states that we have both decided to divorce, we both love and support the children, and we do not want to engage in a shame and blame game? Can we agree that the children do not need to know anything about the reasons the marriage is not working?*

As adults, you need to be on the same page and protect the children from your adult issues. Can you agree that it would be unwise to use the children for your individual emotional support, and you won't do it? The children only need to know that they are safe, loved, and that you as their parents are going to be kind to each other and work things out with the family's needs foremost in your minds.

If you can wait until you have an actual plan in place before telling them, all the better. Children need consistency, and they like plans. If you don't have a common plan yet, maybe it is too early to tell them about the separation because it will contribute to their anxiety and worry. Discuss these things with your co-parenting coach or counselor who is trained in family systems and the effects of divorce.

ONCE SOMEONE DECIDES TO CALL IT QUITS, WHAT NOW?

This is how it often goes: One person in the relationship wants out and has been thinking about it for years. The other person may not have a clue that anything was wrong, or their partner was so unhappy. In my experience, clients often feel compelled to start the legal divorce process before one or both have undergone the psychological divorce. I think this is a huge mistake. That is why I am warning you about this so you can both discuss your options. Often, the person initiating the divorce has been thinking about it for so long, he or she is psychologically ready to be divorced. In fact, now that it is out in the open, they wish they could have been divorced yesterday. In contrast, the other spouse has not had time to process the idea of divorce, let alone the logistics.

It is almost impossible to have a divorce with grace and dignity if one of you insists on jamming the divorce process down the other's throat before both of you have come to terms and acknowledge that the relationship is over. It is unfair to ask your partner for a divorce and then expect him or her to negotiate the most important aspects of life—their children and their financial security—if they haven't had time to realize that a divorce is the best thing to do. This takes time. If you are the person who initiated the divorce, I would urge you to be as patient as you can, despite your certainty that this divorce will happen. It will, I assure you. You will be divorced.

You will be free, and it will be awesome, exhilarating, and scary at times to be on your own. It is also in your own best long-term interests to allow the shocked party to regain his or her bearings. Think about it. How can you negotiate with someone who is right now insane with grief? How will that be anything other than a recipe for disaster, frustration, hurt feelings, and expensive lawyer fees? I am not condoning stonewalling, but there is a difference between shock and denial, and hostile or passive-aggressive stonewalling. Know the difference.

You, the one who is psychologically ready to be divorced, can help by seeking a skilled and experienced mental health professional familiar with collaborative divorce and family system dynamics. You are not seeking counseling to reconcile. You are seeking support to be able to co-parent and move through your divorce with the highest amount of courtesy and respect possible. Hurting your spouse through the weapon of an adversarial divorce will also hurt you and your children. I am not saying that every adversarial divorce is a means to hurt your spouse on purpose. I am saying that the adversarial divorce process is designed to be adversarial. Period. That is how family lawyers are trained.

A courtroom showdown and the adversarial process that leads up to it is where many of us obtain our professional identities and feel our own personal power and validation. Just because the word "family" is in front of the word "court" doesn't make it softer or more empathetic. It's not. It is a court of law.

Ask yourself: *Do you want to be adversaries with the person whom you chose to marry, with whom you were in love, and with whom you chose to have children?* Just think about that question. If your answer is yes, you might as well stop reading now. I have nothing to offer you. If your higher self is at least considering the question, read on.

First Things First: Finding the Right Mental Health Professional

So, if I'm a divorce lawyer, why do I keep harping about mental health issues?

In an ideal situation, when both parties (sorry, that is a term of art; it is how lawyers talk about you when you are not in the room. You are a "party" to the litigation—a plaintiff or a defendant) are both psychologically divorced, then and only then can true negotiations take place that have a chance of meeting everyone's higher needs.

When both people are ready to be divorced, then the children's needs can be placed ahead of the parents' desire for comfort or revenge. Prior to that moment, any attempts at negotiation will be close to futile. Too many emotions are clouding someone's judgment, and the marital dynamic that led to the need for a divorce in the first place will no doubt raise its ugly head throughout the negotiations and at the most inopportune moments.

I often think of the 1970s TV show *Name That Tune*. Some people can name that tune in just a few notes. With a divorce, at times a collaboratively trained colleague and I joke that we could get a couple divorced in about three hours if both clients were psychologically ready. It takes six months to two years because someone is not ready to let go.

Consider this: You may be a year into your adversarial divorce process and find yourselves fighting over some item of personal property. The lawyers are sitting on the other side of the phone at their desks scratching their heads and wondering what the big deal is here. Why are you fighting over this?

Assuming that the lawyers are not causing the impasse, we know that these last-minute conflicts have nothing to do with the personal property or whatever issue is blocking the final resolution. It has everything to do with someone's unwillingness to let go. It has to do with fear. It has to do with emotions, not logic. This is how cases end up in court over principles or punishment. Are you asking the judge to decide who should get the cast-iron baked bean pot or the family pet? Are you trying to squeeze every last nickel out of someone just because you know it will hurt them? If so, then I suggest that you have emotional issues to work through.

Do You Want to Be Devastated, Good Enough, a Competent Loner, or Wholehearted?

During my divorce, I found myself with hours of time on my hands when my daughter was with her father. I'd go to the bookstore searching the self-help materials for how I could get myself through what I found to be the most painful experience of my adult life. I didn't find much help, but I learned about how some people after a divorce are ruined by the experience, some repeat a similar pattern (perhaps several times over, because it is also true that people who have been divorced once have a greater chance of becoming divorced again), some choose to be competent loners whereas others are somehow able to live a wholehearted loving life in partnership with another.[1]

After reading that, I decided that I wanted to be one of the people who could overcome the trauma and drama of a divorce and feel OK, either alone or in partnership with someone new. All I knew for sure was that I did not want to be ruined by this experience, and I sure did not want to repeat the same patterns in a new relationship and call it good enough. I wanted to become openhearted and to learn to not be afraid to love again, at least at some point down the road.

During this time I realized that it was much easier to give good advice to my clients over the years—such as my favorite, "remain above reproach at all times," and "remember, this is a marathon, not a sprint"—than it was to follow that wisdom myself. Going through this process humbled me. I developed even greater empathy for my clients.

If the thought of empathy hasn't crossed your mind recently, I suggest you give it a try. A little empathy for yourself, your partner, and your children during this process will go a long way toward healthy resolution.

IT'S OK: YOUR AMYGDALA HAS BEEN HIJACKED

Sometimes we misinterpret a divorce as a personal moral failing, a reflection that you are no longer wanted or needed by your spouse. This idea of lack of worthiness does something to the brain. It's as if your amygdala has been hijacked. Your fight or flight responses are triggered. You are not thinking with a clear head. You are overwhelmed by fear and anxiety about the future. You may want to obliterate the past and move into your future. You may want to justify or defend your worthiness. You may be unable to even conceive of a future without your spouse and have no ability to let go of the past. You may try to cling to what you thought was your fantasy version of the life you were living. You may want revenge or to hurt your spouse for causing you pain and to punish him or her for this betrayal and injustice. Your negative thoughts might turn inward and manifest as depression, anxiety, or self-harming behavior. Or you may act aggressively toward your spouse or take it out on your children. You are hurt and vulnerable.

TRIAL LAWYERS ARE AWESOME: DO YOU REALLY NEED ONE RIGHT NOW?

This is not the best time to rush to the courthouse unless you need the court's immediate protection from financial fraud, physical or emotional abuse, or you are dealing with severe mental health or substance abuse issues that put yourself or your children in imminent danger.

If you are not in imminent fear of physical or financial abuse, then your first call ought to be the mental health counselor, or a collaborative divorce lawyer, not an adversarial divorce lawyer. Work through the emotions before you try to tackle the legal problems.

Remember, divorce lawyers are trained to fight your battle for you and on your behalf, to get you what you say you want. I'm suggesting that in the early phase of your divorce process you may not have had sufficient time to consider what you *really* want. Divorce lawyers like a challenge, and we enjoy the fight, the sparring, the battle of wits, the drama of a courtroom showdown, and we like to win. We are a competitive bunch.

Civil trial lawyers are your best friend during times of great urgency—when you have been hit by a car and are injured; when you have sustained multiple physical injuries as a result of a product malfunction; when you have lost your job because of discrimination; when an insurance company has refused to compensate you for an accident or negligence of some kind, or perhaps your business copyright is being infringed upon.

Trial lawyers are necessary if you have been a victim of fraud, a crime, or discrimination, or you have been falsely accused of a crime or wrongdoing. I admire trial lawyers and appreciate their value to our society. They help the underdog, the oppressed, the maligned, and they provide people access to our justice system to pursue all available legal remedies regardless of ability to pay up front. Access to justice, the rule of law, and an independent judiciary are fundamental principles of a participatory democracy.

But think about this: The only legal remedy in an adversarial divorce process is a divorce. You will get a decision from a judge about your future financial security and how you will relate to your children throughout their minority. A single piece of paper will declare you divorced. You end up with a copy: no bells, no whistles, no ribbons or fancy seals; just a piece of paper that will incorporate a separate written decision about your money and your children. Do you need a judge to make those decisions for you? Or do you believe that you are capable of making those decisions in your family's best interests even if you need help getting there?

As a divorce lawyer, I am telling you to find the best therapist that you can afford and relate to who will give you honest, objective feedback. Do not find a therapist who will just accept your point of view and join your bandwagon of vitriol and self-justification. Find someone who offers you support and guidance that sounds reasonable to you. You can always change therapists if you don't connect well after a couple of sessions. There is no shame in changing your mind and finding the right people to support you at this early stage of your divorce exploration process.

If you both find mental health professionals, I suspect that you will each come to see the value in slowing down, allowing the emotions to settle, and then you both will be ready and capable of moving toward a civil, even friendly divorce.

WHY DIVORCE IS LIKE A GRIEVING PROCESS (OR NOT)

The reason why I focus on mental health is because getting a divorce is like a grieving process. For years, I have been telling clients that divorce is like a death in the family, except no one is bringing you food.

I hadn't realized how important an early mental health intervention would be in facilitating the legal process. That is why the collaborative divorce model is so attractive and effective. It combines the legal with the psychological for the benefit of the client.

In chapter 8, we explore divorce through the lens of the five common stages of grief described by Elisabeth Kübler-Ross.[2] They are:

1. denial (avoidance, confusion, elation, shock, fear);
2. anger (frustration, irritation, anxiety);
3. bargaining (struggling to find meaning, reaching out to others, sharing one's story and perspective);
4. depression (feeling overwhelmed, helpless, hopeless, hostile, and wanting to run away from the pain); and
5. acceptance (exploring options, putting together a new plan for the future, moving on).

Although never scientifically validated, for purposes of this book divorce as a grieving process seems to fit. In chapter 10, we look at divorce beyond the lens of grief and loss, but from the lens of resiliency, transformation, and an opportunity for personal growth.

DIVORCE IS A COMPLICATED AND CONFUSING TIME OF LIFE

The bottom line in all of this analysis is that divorce is an emotionally complicated time of life. Before you call a shark, call a mental health professional. No one is immune from the emotional toll a divorce has on a family. If you work through the emotional, psychological, and spiritual aspects of divorce, you will eventually come to acceptance. This happens naturally in a collabortive process. At that point, a collaborative divorce lawyer can help you navigate the legal logistics.

Thoughts to Consider

What are my biggest fears? What do I think I know about divorce? Is there a way to do it differently? Is there a way to divorce without a court battle? Can we be friends when this is over? How can we get legal support without costing a fortune or having the lawyer make things worse? How can I find my voice and say what I mean, without saying it meanly?

Thoughts to Let Go

I'll never recover from the shame and embarrassment. I will be ruined emotionally and financially from this process. Our children will suffer because of our divorce.

Practical Tips

Research and preparation are key to a healthy divorce. Think before you speak. First call is to a collaboratively trained lawyer or a mental health professional skilled in family system dynamics and divorce. Learn what to expect from the divorce process, and review all of your options: do it yourself, mediation, collaborative divorce, or litigation.

2

Knowledge Is Power

Is There an Alternative to an Adversarial Divorce?

An adversarial bloodbath will leave you forever wounded, bitter, and resentful. If you think you can "win" an adversarial divorce, I am here to tell you that there is no such thing as a "winner" in family court. You will not emerge unscathed. It is simply not possible. The system itself is designed to be adversarial. It works well if you are injured in an accident and the insurance company is refusing to pay; it works well if you are a multinational company trying to protect your intellectual property from infringement; it works well if you are swindled and a victim of financial fraud. It is a paradigm of civility and due process if you are accused of a crime, and you have sufficient means to hire an attorney.

An adversarial divorce does not work so well if you want to end your marriage with some degree of hope that you and your former spouse will be able to work together for the benefit of your children. It doesn't work so well if you intend to set a positive example for your children for how to handle conflict and adversity in life. It doesn't work so well if you hope to spare your children the pain and emotional burden of listening to your incessant slander of their other parent because they are "taking me to court," . . . "trying to take you away from me," . . . "trying to take all my money," . . . "trying to force us to move out of our home," etc.

The adversarial family court system works if you need it, and it is absolutely necessary to protect you from actual physical abuse, extreme abuse or neglect of children, or imminent financial ruin. Short of that, I suggest that you consider your options.

**Open Your Mind: You Have Options—Representing Yourself
or Using Mediation**

The good news is that divorce is a relatively closed and finite legal
universe. The issues you must consider and resolve are: custody and
a contact schedule with each parent, child support, property division,
and alimony/spousal maintenance. That is it. Take a moment to think
about the types of people you might want help from to figure out the
best resolution to those discrete issues, other than an adversarial lawyer.
Drawing a blank?

Have you considered talking to a skilled child-development specialist who might help you work through the best way to communicate
about the divorce to your children? Or how to set up a parenting plan
that honors both of your parenting styles, given the ages and developmental needs of your children, even if your styles are wildly different?
I've found that when it comes to custody cases, people often assume
that different means wrong or unworthy. Using a professional for help
creates an opening for a divorcing couple to focus on what positive attributes the other parent brings to the children's upbringing, rather than
the adversarial posture of how to keep the other parent at a distance, or
otherwise restrict access between the children and their other parent.
Such a restrictive view often comes into an adversarial divorce because
of a parent's unresolved emotions. Divorce can easily trigger emotional
issues related to rejection, attachment, abandonment, shame, and guilt
or other unresolved trauma. These deeper issues often appear as anger
directed at your spouse. When anger is unresolved, it comes out in a
variety of unhealthy ways, including restricting an otherwise loving and
competent parent from the love and affection of their children.

When it comes to a sensible approach to resolve financial issues,
perhaps it would be wise to consult with a neutral certified financial
divorce analyst/planner who could help you understand your overall
financial situation without selling you any products. This person could
help you both work on your financial disclosure forms, which are required in all divorces. They could help you understand the time value
of money and whether being awarded the marital home is really in your
financial interests.

A quick heads-up: The financial disclosure process is a place where
divorce lawyers make a lot of money because it is time consuming
and tedious. It also has an uncanny effect of intimidating a witness or
overwhelming him. Formally, the process is called "discovery." In the

adversarial model, each of you is entitled to "discover" the financial data of the other person (think about producing the past 5–10 years of all of your financial records, bank records, credit cards, insurance policies, retirement accounts, etc.). A process governs discovery. It may involve multiple questions including subparts about every account in which you have had any interest for many years, sometimes up to the length of time of the marriage. It is invasive and time consuming. It produces hundreds (sometimes thousands) of pages of documents. These documents need to be read and organized by your lawyer, their paralegal or associate. This takes time and money. Often, the lawyers may object to production of certain documents and not produce the ones your lawyer wants to use to help prove a theory of the case. These objections need to be resolved in some manner.

The rules of court procedure require that before the attorney may file a motion to compel production and ask for sanctions for failing to provide the requested information, the lawyers need to demonstrate that they have made a good faith effort to resolve the issue between themselves before filing for relief from the court. That will usually require at least two letters between the lawyers. This takes time and costs money. If the lawyers can't work it out, then someone files a motion (a request) with the court. Then the other party files a response. This takes time and money.

Eventually, you will get a court date to address the outstanding discovery issues. You will need to take time off from work to appear and argue to the court about why the lawyers couldn't work out financial disclosures between them. This takes time and money. Remember: every hour of court time takes about seven hours of preparation. Eventually, you will get a decision. Either the information will be produced, or there will be some limitation on production.

In my experience, the court always makes an effort to appear even-handed, so no one ever wins everything he asks for, and both litigants usually walk away feeling slightly, if not royally, dissatisfied. I call this the "pox on both of your houses" syndrome.

Once "discovery" has been completed, then there is an opportunity to resolve the case between the lawyers, by exchanging written proposals. These offers of settlement are confidential, and you can't use the offers in court later on if you don't resolve the case by agreement. Statistically, 98 percent of cases settle. If direct negotiation by letter doesn't work, then the next step is mediation, which I'll describe in detail below. If mediation doesn't work, then you will be set for a final contested hearing with the court. When your lawyer says that you will need two days—or two weeks—to put on your evidence, remember: one hour of court time costs seven hours of preparation. Also, the courts are so overbooked that the time between your request and a final hearing date may be many months down the road.

During this waiting time, it is likely that your relationship with your spouse probably will get worse, and tensions between you probably will rise. There is no encouragement that you two start some post-separation counseling to learn how to stop hating each other. If that were encouraged, you probably wouldn't need a contested divorce.

At this point you may be sent to mediation. Mediation is another route to divorce that does not involve going to trial. I will also explain what to expect if you represent yourself, how the collaborative divorce process works, and what to expect from the litigation process.

REPRESENTING YOURSELF: PROS AND CONS

I teach the "pro se" education class in Vermont's family courts. Pro se means "on your own"—as in, no lawyer, but still choosing to engage in the adversarial process. Many people today represent themselves because they lack the financial resources to retain counsel, or they are scared that the lawyers will upset the delicate balance you have managed to create with your soon-to-be former spouse. I'll go over the basics of what I share with the pro se ed class. It is still not a substitute for actual legal advice, and every state has a different set of laws on domestic relations, child custody and support, and division of property and alimony. You should definitely go online and download your state's laws on these subjects (or go to your state's judiciary home page, where perhaps the family law forms and information are available for you to review). It is important to have a sense of the legal framework in which to discuss these issues with your spouse and know what to expect from your jurisdiction (i.e., the place you live and where your divorce will be legally and formally resolved).

Even after you attempt to educate yourself about the basics from the information that your state offers, you can also call a lawyer to help explain areas of confusion. Most lawyers will offer a free half-hour consultation. Remember, a single lawyer cannot represent both of you, because of the potential (some might say likelihood) for a conflict of interest. This is true, even if you and your spouse "agree on everything." We just can't do it in our capacity as attorneys. On occasion, I have acted as a neutral consultant to explain the basics of the system to a couple, or I have served as a mediator. If I am consulting about process issues and options, I am always careful not to get into the specifics of the case, and I do not give actual legal advice. I just share information that they could find if they did what I am suggesting they do: research the law of domestic relations in your state to educate yourself about which factors the courts consider in a custody case; which factors apply to dividing the property and alimony; and how child support is calculated, for example. What the online forms won't explain, however, is some of the more subtle nuances for you to consider, or what to do if you can't agree on the value of an asset, for example, or whether your state is an equitable distribution state, a community property state, or a separate property state. This is where consulting with a family law attorney could help you, without taking over your case.

Representing yourself has its pros and cons. On the pro side, it gives you a lot of autonomy and it is the least expensive option. On the con side, you are not a lawyer, and yet you will be expected by the court system to behave as if you were.

Here's how a typical case moves through the family court system: In Vermont, it starts when someone files a summons and complaint for divorce. One person is the plaintiff and the other the defendant. It doesn't matter who files first, and just because you are the defendant in the case, doesn't mean you are considered the bad guy or the person at fault. Divorce cases are civil in nature, as opposed to criminal. It is just part of the adversarial process that the first one to the courthouse to file the complaint is the "plaintiff," and the other person is the "defendant." The defendant then has to file an answer to the complaint and, usually, a counterclaim for divorce.

Once the answer is filed, the case receives a docket number. This number is how the court keeps track of your papers. Everything you send to the court (i.e., "file") should have the docket number on it, and you have to send a copy to the other side.

You may have a court-ordered class or two to attend. In Vermont, if you are going to represent yourself, you must take the hour-long pro se education class, and if you have children, you must take a class about helping children cope with the effects of divorce. It is four hours long; you must pay a fee for the class, and it is mandatory. While a parenting class might seem onerous, it can be a helpful reminder to put the effect the divorce is having on your children at the forefront of your minds. If your state offers or requires such a class, I recommend that you both sign up for it immediately and go together so that you hear the same information at the same time. You may obtain a certificate of attendance so that you have proof that you took the class.

Usually, you will be required to attend a case manager conference. The case manager is there as an early monitor to assess whether you are able to reach an agreement or whether you will need court time to resolve your dispute, whether it is about custody, temporary possession of the home, temporary support (child and/or spousal), payment of the bills upon separation, etc. The case manager conference comes up relatively quickly, and some pressure is put upon you to "settle" the issues. (It is safe to say that all family courts across the country are overburdened with cases, the judiciary budgets are insufficient to meet the needs of the people, there are not enough judges or staff, and court time is at a premium. Hence the rise of mandatory mediation.)

If you reach an agreement, congratulations. You are done. If you have met the six-month waiting period (or other mandatory waiting periods) required for divorcing people with children, then you will simply be set for a final uncontested hearing to get divorced when that mandatory waiting period has been met. An uncontested hearing is one where you present the court with your agreement, you identify yourselves, you testify to your residence, marriage, separation, and grounds for the divorce. (Usually in a no-fault state, it is because you have lived separate and apart for more than six months and it is unlikely that you will resume your marital relationship.) Other grounds for divorce include adultery, intolerable severity, or lunacy. But the typical divorce is the "no fault," or irreconcilble type of divorce.

In Vermont, most people use the no-fault grounds for divorce, as no financial advantage accrues to filing under any other grounds—alleging adultery, for example, may make you feel better temporarily by calling out your ex in a public document, but it doesn't translate into more money. At the uncontested final hearing you present your previously agreed-upon settlement on custody and property/alimony, and you get divorced that day or when the judge signs it. You can request to resume use of your former name as well if you took the last name of your spouse at marriage. This saves you the trouble of going through a more formal procedure in probate court to change your name. If you change your name, remember that you will still have to change it through the Social Security Administration, the Department of Motor Vehicles, your bank, and anywhere else you use your name. Many people prefer to keep the same last name as their children. If you want to use your former name, then ask a lawyer in your jurisdiction about ways to do that.

If you are unable to resolve the custody and/or support issues, the case manager will set you up for a status conference with the court. This is a time when you advise the judge of the issues you are fighting about, and you explain how much time you will need for an evidentiary hearing. Sometimes the court may change something about your status quo at a status conference, even though you were not expecting to have a hearing. This can be an unsettling experience, but it does happen.

An evidentiary hearing is one where you will present evidence. Evidence is your testimony (the words you say under oath in front of the judge), and it may be documentary as well (documents that confirm what you say or contradict what the other person says). This is where people may invoke their stereotypes of courtroom TV law shows. You may "object" to testimony that is based upon hearsay (any out-of-court statement offered to prove the truth of the matter asserted). There are a host of rules about evidence: what comes in, what must stay out. It is technical, and it takes lawyers many years to understand and apply correctly. When you represent yourself, you are held to the same standard of practice as a lawyer, even though you have not gone to law school, and you are emotionally invested in the outcome of your case. That can be a tough combination.

At a status conference (sometimes called a "calendar call"), a court may inquire whether you have attempted mediation. If you haven't, then it is likely the court will send you to mediation before you will get court time to present your facts, evidence, and arguments. Presenting a custody case, or a division of property/alimony case is not easy for most lawyers, so I can imagine that it will not be easy for you either. If you are heading to a contested case, I strongly urge you to consult with an attorney to make sure that you are presenting the type of relevant and reliable information the court will need to apply the law to your facts. How to try a case in court is beyond the scope of this book. I will explain to you, however, what a mediator is and how collaborative divorce and/or mediation are models available to you.

WHAT IS A MEDIATOR, AND HOW DO I USE ONE?

Once you have worked through the emotional aspects of your separation, and there has been full disclosure of the family finances, you are now equipped to engage in a careful discussion about your future relationship with your children and your financial security. I suggest that regardless of how well you think you are getting along up to this point, this will still be a difficult conversation. It will likely trigger old feelings, doubts, and insecurities. It is probably wise to use a neutral third party, such as a mediator, to facilitate this conversation. Even if you are not getting along, if you are still stuck in the emotional quagmire, or even actively involved in litigation, you may still be required to attend a mediation, so I'll explain what it is and how it works.

A mediator is a person who has received education and training in the art of facilitating a difficult conversation and deconstructing conflict. Mediators are neutral. They cannot give legal advice (even if the mediator is also a lawyer). They help you and the person with whom you are in a dispute have an open and honest conversation with the goal of reaching an agreement, if you want one. The mediator has no skin in the game. Mediators would like to help you reach a resolution, but if you don't, they are not emotionally invested in your outcome.

Mediations are confidential. What is said during a mediation cannot be used against you in court. You cannot subpoena the mediator (a subpoena is a formal process to compel someone into court to testify).

Mediation is an excellent choice if you are looking to represent yourself and you feel like it would be a good idea to have someone neutral facilitate the conversation so that you don't fall into old habits and patterns of communication that leave you feeling like your head might explode. The presence of a neutral can help you bring about a peaceful resolution that meets your needs, so long as you know in advance what those needs are.

Often mediation is a way to retain a high degree of control over your dispute resolution process at a modest financial cost. This model is most appropriate for a couple on relatively equal footing when it comes to assertiveness and bargaining power. If the dynamic of your marriage was such that you always said yes, or always deferred to whatever your spouse suggested, then mediation (without a lawyer) may not be the most appropriate dispute resolution option for you. If you have no idea about the finances of your marital estate because you always deferred to your spouse, then you need to ask yourself: *How much do I trust my spouse's integrity and honesty to disclose all of the financial information and be an accurate reporter of the facts?* If you trust, then mediation is still a good option.

If your reaction to that last question was something like "What? No, I don't trust! Are you kidding me?," then, I'd say mediation should not be your first step toward resolution. In order to negotiate a deal for yourself through mediation, you need to be highly confident that you know the facts of your marital estate. That means the value of all of your assets and liabilities, joint, sole, or mixed. You need to assess the fair market value of your home, your "big ticket" personal property (boats, cars, special collections of any kind). You need to see a bank statement, a retirement account statement; you may be entitled to a marital portion of an old-school pension, IRA, 401(k), 403(b), or other retirement/investment account, even if it is in your spouse's name.

Do you live in a community property state, where your marital assets will be divided 50/50; or an equitable distribution state, where the court has discretion to divide your marital estate, based upon a list of factors? That is a good question for a free consultation with a lawyer, or a quick Google search, if you don't know the answer already.

Do some "footwork" before you go to mediation, because you can't mediate a settlement if you don't know the underlying value of your marital estate. You could mediate issues regarding the children and then go back once you have collected your data and, hopefully, spoken with an attorney to understand the law of property division and spousal support (alimony) in your jurisdiction. Once you have done that, you will be ready for a mediation.

A note about personal property: This is a weirdly emotional issue. I'm just giving you advance notice of this fact. People spend a lot of time and energy on how to divide the personal property. If this is a sore spot for you or your spouse, give it some time before you try to tackle it. I generally see resistance about personal property as symbolic of not being ready to "let go."

Some people want to value all of their personal property, down to the stuff in the drawers in the kitchen. I am not a fan of the "let's put a value on every item of personal property in the house," because, frankly, the value is what you would get for it if you sold it at a garage sale. It is not replacement value, or even what you paid for it. So, you could come up with an arbitrary figure for the "value" of the items remaining in the home, but that is a tedious exercise if you cannot agree upon that figure. It is easier to simply agree on who takes what, but if you can't agree, then the court is there to listen to you.

Yes, it will cost money to set up a second house for the person leaving (unless you sell the house and all of its contents and split it all evenly). I prefer to assess the cost of setting up a new place and factor that into the final analysis, rather than dwelling on how to value the Tupperware, linens, furniture, appliances, and so forth, in the house.

I am not saying taking a good inventory and having a ballpark value isn't reasonable; it is. Just try not to get too sidetracked in the minutiae of personal property, or get bogged down in thinking about the "unfairness" that one of you "gets to buy all new things" and the other doesn't. It all works out in the end. Yes, maybe the moving spouse does get some new stuff, but that person is moving out of his or her home, because your marriage isn't working anymore. A few new things are a small comfort compared to the loss of a marriage and a home that was built together over many years, regardless of the reason the marriage is ending. It is still a huge loss, for both of you. Try to keep that in mind, untangle your "stuff," and look forward to a fresh start.

I've seen many negotiations get bogged down in the valuation of miscellaneous personal property. If you sense that will happen to you, hire an auction house to give you an expert neutral opinion about the value of the stuff. Of course, if you have a fancy collection, or you think something of value should be assessed, then you can hire a certified appraiser who specializes in that area. This is usually a cost that should be shared between you as part of the expense of getting divorced. Even if you think it is stupid to spend the money on an appraiser, just do it. It will save you thousands of dollars down the road when the lawyers have to get involved.

There are different types of mediations and mediators. It is important to understand the options within the field of mediation and to ask for the type of mediation that will serve you best. Remember, if your mediator is a lawyer, he is not there to provide "legal advice" but he can help explain the issues that will need to be resolved. He can also help you draft your agreement. A good mediator will urge you both to consult with independent counsel before you sign off on a legally binding document. The mediator is not there to represent either one of you and will be prohibited ethically from doing so after the mediation ends.

MEDIATION WITHOUT LAWYERS

Mediation without lawyers present can be an economical and empowering process. Done correctly, it is an invitation to sit down with your spouse, in a safe and confidential setting, to have a difficult but productive conversation about your divorce. Before sitting down to mediate your divorce, I strongly encourage you to at least seek the guidance of an experienced family law attorney who supports mediation. You can't really go wrong looking for lawyers who advertise that they practice collaborative divorce *and* are members of the International Academy of Collaborative Professionals (IACP)—you can be reasonably confident that they talk the talk and walk the walk of a non-adversarial divorce process. This initial contact can be quite valuable to you so that you understand what you can negotiate and what you cannot. For example, you cannot negotiate your values or your feelings. You can negotiate interests. Learn the difference.

Keep in mind that if you do not have a lawyer at the outset of your mediation with whom you would like to form an attorney-client relationship, you should keep looking until you find the right one for you. Sometimes a lawyer will send you to mediation without her, but then when you show up with the "mediated agreement," the lawyer will point out the flaws and may undermine the effort you just made to get an agreement that you thought was reasonable. I suggest that you go into the mediation with an idea of reasonableness, rather than learning after the fact that what you just spent hours of time and emotional energy creating was not in your best long-term interests.

CONCEPTS AND TERMS TO KNOW IN ADVANCE

Mediator: A neutral third party to help you reach a resolution. A mediator can be a lawyer by profession or someone who specializes in dispute resolutions. It doesn't matter unless you want your mediator to help with extra tasks such as drafting your mediation agreement, helping you put your agreement into a legally acceptable format, helping with the additional paperwork necessary for filing your divorce in court, or helping you look for an "evaluative" mediation.

Mediation Format: Shuttle diplomacy versus sitting in the same room. In traditional civil litigation, a model was developed for shuttle diplomacy where the clients and their lawyers are in separate rooms for most of the mediation (after an initial opening statement). The mediator goes between the rooms with offers and counter-offers. It involves a lot of down time when the mediator is visiting with the other side. Be prepared.

If there are no lawyers or safety concerns (e.g., domestic violence, active addiction issues), then the mediator might conduct the entire mediation with you and your spouse sitting in the same room and talking through the issues.

Evaluative Mediation: This type of mediation is more common in civil disputes, such as car accidents or personal injury, or other claims where lawyers typically are involved. Lawyers will choose an experienced lawyer who will also serve as the mediator. The hope is that the mediator/lawyer will give some reality checking to the lawyers and parties about the merits of the claim and what an objectively reasonable settlement would look like.

In my mediation practice, I use this approach. I think it is important for clients to understand whether their proposal is objectively reasonable.

All agreements must still be approved by a judge, who has an independent obligation to ensure that all agreements are objectively reasonable. Sometimes, people who represent themselves (*pro se*) may still need to go to court to explain in person to a judge why they agreed to what they did because it doesn't look fair or reasonable to the judge. Upon hearing your explanation, the court may accept it or reject it; if rejected you may be encourage to seek legal counsel.

Shuttle Diplomacy: This is a form of mediation. You and your spouse do not even sit in the same room with one another but in separate rooms. It is usually the idea of one of your lawyers. It is time consuming. The mediator goes back and forth between you in an effort to get you to an agreement. It can mean many minutes of just sitting in the room, waiting for the mediator to come back with the latest "position." If active domestic abuse is involved, this type of mediation is usually not an option. This form of mediation works to get a deal, but it may not be the best model if you hope to heal old wounds and wounds, and improve communication with your spouse.

Shuttle diplomacy is often used when lawyers are involved, and one lawyer "insists" that the clients be separated. The lawyer who does this is not helping to create an environment where you and your soon-to-be former spouse can learn to communicate effectively with each other for a healthier post-marriage relationship.

Sometimes a person will claim that they "cannot" sit in the same room together. I say, "try harder and get over yourself." I understand that it is not comfortable, but growth comes at the edge of discomfort. I'm not talking about situations where abuse—physical, emotional, or otherwise—is involved. I'm just saying that a little discomfort now for a long-term, peaceful, dignified resolution free of bitterness and resentment is worth the effort.

If you can't see yourself being able to sit in the same room with the other parent of your children, then now is the time to go to post-separation counseling (either together or by yourself) to learn to express yourselves honestly. If you have never been to therapy, then I suggest starting there, for yourself. If you have some insight and have been in therapy before, then finding a post-separation communication coach might be a good idea. However you do it, start to work through your anger, resentment, and poor communication or whatever led to the divorce in the first place.

If you are not capable of sitting in a room together to negotiate the end of your marriage, then you still have emotional work to do before you tackle the daunting task of getting divorced. You can do it. You may need support along the way, but collaboratively trained lawyers can help. They understand the complex emotional issues and will not rush you into an adversarial divorce. It is no shame to admit that you need time to deal with your emotional response to ending your relationship. I think that is fair and not too much to ask of yourself, your spouse, or your lawyers.

MEDITATION WITH LAWYERS—
A CONTINUUM OF OPTIONS

Role of Lawyers: A lawyer could assist in a noninvasive way to help educate you about your state's domestic relations law. The lawyer can sit with you and charge you by the hour to help you understand and navigate your mediation. The lawyer can educate you in advance about how courts in your state divide property, calculate child support and/or alimony; and can assess some boundaries of what would constitute a reasonable settlement. Lawyers know what would pass muster with the court and what would be considered lopsided or unfair.

The most common type of mediator is a nonlawyer who will help you identify your goals and interests. Goals and interests are different from positions. For example, consider these statements: I want alimony. I want sole custody of the children. I want the house. I want to be debt free. I want my spouse to suffer as much as possible. Just kidding. I added that last one to make sure you are still paying attention.

Now consider these statements: I need sufficient financial security to live a comfortable life. I want to live in a place that is safe and convenient for the children. I want to have a positive relationship with my children, see them frequently, and be involved in decisions that will impact their future.

The former statements are positions. The latter are interests.

A story I heard once describes the difference between a position and an interest. A parent overhears the children fighting loudly over an orange. The parent, fed up with the bickering and crying steps in with what she thinks is the solution. She takes the orange and simply cuts it in half and gives each child half of the orange. This does not stop the crying. Rather, it intensifies.

What is the problem? the parent thinks. *They each got half the orange?* The parent steps back a moment, takes a deep breath, and asks an honest and open question. "What is it that you wanted?" One child says she is hungry and wants to eat the orange; the other says he wants the rind for a project he is working on. So now, the parent who jumped in with a solution the children in dispute did not want or ask for has created a situation in which neither child is satisfied. And the one who wanted the rind is even more upset because his interest cannot be met at all at this point. The moral of the story: Take a deep breath and ask curious questions to understand what is underlying their stated positions. Each child wanted the orange, but for different purposes. A mediator would have been able to assess the underlying interests by asking the children to explain what they truly wanted and needed so that they could hear each other and come up with a solution that best fit their needs. A little listening goes a long way.

A traditional mediator does not give answers or tell you what to do. Mediators are not judges, so they do not make decisions. They are not serving as lawyers, so they do not provide legal advice. Even if your mediator is also an attorney licensed to practice law, the role of the lawyer in mediation is as a mediator, not an advice giver. A specific type of mediation is practiced by lawyers in civil litigation in which a mediator/lawyer acts as a neutral evaluator. I described that above, but assuming you are sticking with the single mediator model, these folks should be skilled in creating a safe, neutral, and confidential space for a conversation about challenging issues or conflicts. It is up to you and your spouse to come up with solutions. The solutions will not be imposed upon you.

The mediator in this type of model is not interested in whether you reach a resolution, but in creating an environment and a process for you to resolve your problems. Depending on your level of motivation and the motivation of your spouse, you may or may not be able to reach a resolution in that first session.

Mediation can last as long as you need; typically, it seems like two hours together is usually enough to at least start the conversation and reach some understandings. Going much longer is emotionally draining, and clarity of thought starts to fade as hunger and exhaustion start to creep in. Just so you know, some mediations are practically marathons: they can go on for four, six, eight, or ten hours.

I am not a fan of that model for divorcing couples. In my experience that model usually involves lawyers on both sides. The case has been going for many months, if not years, and has been adversarial from the start. The case is probably about to go to trial, and the court or the lawyers think that maybe now they should try to settle it. The adversarial model has resulted in months of intentionally separating you and your spouse from working through the emotional issues in your divorce. This type of marathon mediation usually occurs on the eve of a contested custody or property division case and feels like a last-ditch effort to reach a resolution short of a fully contested trial.

In that model, the ultimate resolution usually is reached out of sheer exhaustion rather than a true sense of ownership of the outcome. This model is disempowering and expensive for clients. It does not encourage positive, direct communication between you and your spouse.

How much you can resolve in a single session will depend entirely on where you are in the grieving process. If you are coming to mediation early in your process when emotions are still running hot, mediation is more challenging, as you can imagine. You may need to tackle "pressing concerns" to start with and schedule a follow-up or two as time allows. If you have had time to grieve your losses and have been managing pretty well, and it seems like it is time to formalize your status quo, then mediation can be an excellent and inexpensive model to use.

Mediation works when you do not have too much to fight about, and division of your marital estate is not overly complicated. Mediators should always refer you to an attorney to review any summary or actual agreements reached during mediation. If they don't, do not sign anything without having a divorce lawyer that you trust review the agreement with you. Sometimes divorce lawyers will notice issues that you didn't think about, or they might suggest that you could've done better for yourself if you had hired them. That may be true, but it may not matter. If you feel comfortable with the agreement you reached during mediation, then you can stick with your gut feeling and move forward.

Just because a divorce lawyer tells you that you could have done better does not mean that your agreement isn't within the realm of reasonableness. You are looking for a resolution that is reasonable and meets your needs. If the lawyer says that your agreement is fundamentally unreasonable, unfair, unconscionable, unenforceable, or otherwise so wrong that it belies credibility, then listen to your lawyer and try again. It may be that you were too vulnerable or unprepared for the mediation in the first place, and that model was not appropriate for you at that time.

But if the issue is simply that the lawyer could have gotten you a slightly better deal, then engage in a risk/benefit/cost analysis and assess how much money you would need to spend to get that extra bump. Is it worth it: For the money? For the peace? For your kids to watch you engage in an adversarial process? It is a fair question, and one you should take the time to consider.

Thoughts to Consider

If a collaborative divorce process doesn't suit my needs, what other option makes the most sense? Do I understand the risks and benefits of the different options? Is my case relatively simple? Do I feel like I have equal bargaining power? Do I know all of the facts? Do I trust my spouse enough to believe they will honestly disclose assets and liabilities? Would consulting with a lawyer before mediation help me feel prepared?

Thoughts to Let Go

I hate my spouse; my spouse caused this mess. I'll never recover from this experience. I will be ruined financially and emotionally, and so will our children. Is my case relatively simple? Do I feel on even footing to bargain with my spouse? Do I know all the facts, or do I trust my spouse to honestly disclose the information I need to make an informed choice if I don't know it? Would a consultation with a lawyer help me prepare for a mediation?

Practical Tips

Understand what to expect from the different options: do-it-yourself, mediation, collaborative divorce, and litigation. Make an informed choice based upon your needs, budget, and interests.

3

Find a Lawyer You Can Trust
Good Lawyers Are Worth Their Weight in Gold

My theory is that lawyers and clients are either peas in a pod, or the lawyer is the client's alter ego.

Now, of course, I am biased in favor of people having competent lawyers on their side from the moment you contemplate a divorce. I'm a divorce lawyer. This is what I do for a living. I understand that you need to feel secure and supported, and you want to know your rights. I can explain the law and tell you about your options, all of them, because I have practiced in all three aspects of family law: adversarial, mediation, and collaborative divorce.

You need to ask yourself: Do I want to be in a pod with this lawyer? Or do I need this lawyer to be my warrior, my knight, my voice, because I cannot find my voice right now? Personally, I don't have a preference, although I do like to know in advance what you expect of me. If you need support, and you want me to help you find your voice, and while you are working on that, act as your proxy, I'm good with that.

If we are more kindred in spirit and more like peas in a pod, then I need to both like and trust you, as much as you like and trust me. I had a business coach scold me for this concept. He argued that clients don't need to like me, and I don't need to like them to get the job done. Fair enough. That is true from a strictly business, bottom line, billable hour point of view.

But as a collaborative divorce attorney, I want to know that I am making a positive contribution to the betterment of your overall life. I'd hope you would want me to bring my full experience as a lawyer and a human being to the relationship as I help you move through this major life transition.

In order to maintain my sense of purpose and joy, then I need to work with people I like and respect. I also want that to be reciprocated by my client, because ours is a relationship of trust that is being developed over time. Yes, of course, you are paying for my expertise, guidance, and counsel. You need it, and I have it to offer. But for lawyers with busy practices, we don't need you as a client, especially if our practice is already full of people we like and want to help. We have a choice whether to take your case. You can also afford to be picky about the lawyer you choose as well. This is not brain surgery, where the bedside manner of your doctor is irrelevant to you, because you just need the surgery to be precise and successful so that you don't die.

A divorce is more like a metaphoric death that provides you with an opportunity to transform your life; to experience the pain of grief and loss, then to have time to get your head together so you can emerge healthy and wholehearted, not bitter and resentful. I think a combination of both personality and skills matters; and you need to find a "good fit," because your relationship with your divorce attorney is likely to be intense, and it usually lasts for six months to a year or more.

Divorce lawyers learn everything about you and your marriage. You pay us a lot of money, and we do our best to represent your interests at a time of your life when you may not even know what you what or who you are anymore. That's the first thing.

Second, a good divorce lawyer should empower you to find your voice through this process. You will need it after the divorce is over. Why? Because the lawyer walks away, having been paid (or not), and you may still be required to engage with your former spouse, especially if you have children, or if you wish to maintain relationships with extended family or friends in your community. The myth of divorce is that you won't have to deal with your ex anymore, and I'm sorry to say, that is just not reality. And folks who choose a collaborative divorce understand this both intuitively and cognitively.

It is common for traditional divorce lawyers to end up with massive receivables because the time commitment is huge, the initial intake may not have revealed the complexity of the case or the dynamic between you and your spouse and, well, because litigation is expensive. This makes for cranky, cynical divorce lawyers.

Divorce lawyers, especially if we have not been trained in collaborative practice, view our role as limited to do the job (i.e., apply the facts to the law, present the case, get paid, and move on to the next client) without much reflection or concern about how the adversarial process eviscerated any chance of post-divorce peace and happiness for you and your family, friends, and community. Also, you should know that statistically, if your divorce ends up in front of a judge for a contested case, you are far more likely to be embroiled in ongoing, post-divorce litigation until your children become adults. It is a heartbreaking but avoidable outcome if you are pro-active now and consider the possibility of changing course and choosing the collaborative model.

Part of the reason for many post-judgment problems (i.e., after the divorce process is over, you or your spouse return to court) is that you completely delegated the decision making for what might work for your family to a judge who does not know you and will never have enough time to fully understand your situation. Judges do the best they can in an overburdened system. They hear truly awful stories all day long. The court's solution will never be as nuanced or helpful as an agreement that you were involved in creating. Period. That is why in the collaborative model, we put the emphasis back on you and your spouse to work together, with the team, to generate ideas and solutions that will be durable and long-lasting.

Research shows that collaborative divorce agreements are less likely to end up in court down the road. The reason is that the time, energy, and effort that you put into a collaborative process pay off in the end. It is not an easy process, but it is often more satisfying to take responsibility for your divorce than to hand it over to the adversarial process and hope that it turns out OK for you.

A LITTLE BIT MORE ABOUT DIVORCE LAWYERS

I'm often taken aback when clients tell me that they were so nervous to meet me the first time we spoke. I forget that talking to a lawyer is not something most people ever do in their lives (unless they are buying a home or running a business, for example) and most hope never to meet a lawyer if they can help it. So, when divorce shows up in their lives, they are not excited to meet me. Often people are scared, anxious, and nervous to even talk with an attorney, even when they know or should know that what they say is completely confidential. I thought it would be useful to share some of my thoughts about what to expect from lawyers and how to approach your relationship with your divorce lawyer.

I am proud to be an ethical, principled, kind, helpful, and competent lawyer. Lawyers get a bad rap in the press and in society. It's been that way for a while (think of Shakespeare's "First, we kill all the lawyers"). Really, that's not nice.

I only ask that you think twice before being mean to a lawyer, especially a divorce lawyer. We have tremendous responsibilities on our shoulders to help you in your most vulnerable time. I am not judging, but whatever you did to get yourself involved with one of us is your responsibility, not ours. You need to admit that you made some poor choices somewhere along that relationship continuum. It's OK. People make mistakes. You made a mistake. I made a mistake. It happens. However, you are not a victim (even if you have been abused . . . you are still a survivor, and you still have choices to make . . . always).

My theory about divorce lawyers and their clients being "peas in a pod" or your "alter ego" is based on my observations over time that clients seem drawn to their lawyer because they feel sympatico with them, or because they need their lawyer to do or say what they fear they cannot. In a traditional divorce, a timid person may be drawn to a stronger bully of a lawyer for fear of not being heard. A high-energy or super-intense person might be drawn to a calmer-souled lawyer to feel some balance and to be able to act as a counterweight.

In a collaborative divorce process, the lawyers and the clients have a similar baseline—they want an efficient, friendly process, without gamesmanship, where they can walk away and feel OK. No one feels great during or immediately after a divorce, but the collaborative divorce process at least offers an opportunity to set the bar a little bit higher than the norm.

Knowing your spouse as you do, think about how you might want to avoid dealing with two of them. If you follow the guidance of this book and search for a non-adversarial model to work through your current problems like a grown-up, you have a better chance of not engaging the fight with your spouse, who then hires a lawyer who appears to be just like your spouse but with a law degree and license to take you to court.

Divorce lawyers are a fascinating group. My theory about us goes something like this: Most of us were drawn to practicing family law because we want to help and be of service. I believe that. People don't choose randomly to practice family law. It takes a special person to do this work every day for years at a time. At our core, we want to be useful and helpful. We are also a competitive lot. We are smart, bold, and professionally trained to be zealous advocates. Lawyers all swear an oath to uphold our professional ethics, which require us to be "zealous advocates" for our clients. The term "zealous" has been modified in some states' ethics rules over the years, because lawyers have taken the word "zealous" a bit too far sometimes.

Lawyers who are not family and divorce lawyers often think we are "weird" or "really brave." Before I started practicing law, family cases were handled in superior court; "family courts" didn't exist. Family courts were a bit of an experiment, with the good intention of having a specialized court where issues of child custody, child support, property division, and alimony could be resolved. The superior court could then handle the other "serious" matters (i.e., personal injury, discrimination, civil rights, products liabilities, medical malpractice, etc.). I have heard that in some places, in the early days, divorces were done by a jury trial. Can you imagine having your marital conflicts on display for a group of your neighbors to decide your fate?

Although a jury will no longer decide your divorce, a divorce court is still a public matter, and anyone is free to view and copy most of the documents that are filed in court. The public is allowed to come and watch your case. Only juvenile cases (abuse and neglect, or delinquency) and mental health cases are confidential and not open to the public, although local practices may vary.

Over the years, I've observed a hierarchy within the legal profession that not all lawyers are alike. I see the hierarchy something like this: There are trial lawyers and there are transactional lawyers. Transactional lawyers take care of things outside of the courtroom: They draft documents and contracts; negotiate deals and provide advice to businesses, schools, and nonprofits; deal with estate plans and other legal formalities.

Trial lawyers are the ones transactional lawyers call when it hits the fan: when the contract is broken; when someone is seriously injured in an accident; when someone dies as a result of malpractice or negligence; when someone is a victim of consumer fraud or any other cause of action that would permit an injured person to recover money. Then trial lawyers are the ones you need.

Trial lawyers also work for insurance companies. Regardless of who employs them, trial lawyers are masters of the courtroom and become masters of the subject matter of the cases they are trying. It often doesn't matter what the subject of the litigation is; a trial lawyer will become an expert in the subject for the trial. Their job requires them to engage in an adversarial system with arcane and complex rules of procedure and evidence.

Most cases settle. However, if the case doesn't settle, then the trial lawyer puts all of her energy and resources together with a team of support people. This preparation will lead to an ultimate showdown in a courtroom. It may involve a jury. The lawyers present their client's case in a way that is supposed to be persuasive, to allow the judge or jury to discern the truth.

A civil jury trial between two worthy adversaries is a beautiful thing to witness, and it is an incredible thing to experience as an attorney. It requires a tremendous amount of preparation and skill to do it well. I really admire trial lawyers. They are tough, no-nonsense, smart, skillful, and often brutal gladiators for their client's cause.

Then there are criminal trial lawyers. I absolutely love these folks. They are the bedrock of democracy. The fact that we are presumed innocent until proven guilty is a cornerstone of our system of justice, and it is a system worthy of respect and awe. Public defenders do their jobs to protect our most sacred constitutional rights, such as our right to an attorney if we cannot afford one; our right to be free from unreasonable search and seizure; our right to confront witnesses against us; our right to a jury trial; our right to not incriminate ourselves and to make the state with all of its superior resources and power prove its case to a jury of our peers beyond a reasonable doubt before our liberty may be taken.

The system is certainly not perfect as we see the ongoing challenge of dismantling institutional racism and the imprisonment of a disproportionate number of African Americans in private, for-profit prisons.[1]

Back to family lawyers. Relative to the rest of the bar, not that many of us are out there. Most lawyers, even criminal lawyers, do not like to practice family law and would not do it even if you paid them a lot of money. It is too stressful, too emotional, and sometimes it is hard to discern whether the rules of evidence even apply.

Like criminal lawyers, family lawyers who represent parents of minor children deal with serious constitutional rights, such as the right to relate to your children free from unwarranted governmental interference. Divorce laws are primarily state driven, not federal. So, even if you don't have children, and if it is not a constitutional issue, you still have a vested interest in your property, your income, your retirement, and your basic human right to live the life you choose to live, married or not.

In collaborative cases, we use a divorce coach to work through issues related to communication about children, whether they are minors or adults. Whether or not you have children, we use a financial neutral to collect and analyze the marital estate, however that is defined in your local jurisdiction. We talk about division of income, assets, and liabilities.

These conversations often bring up a host of feelings, and the strength of the collaborative divorce container provides you with the time and space you need to work through the emotional aspects before we start to generate options for settlement.

In contrast, in a traditional adversarial case, we put all the issues in front of a judge to decide. Regardless of the model, family lawyers work with you when you are not at your best (see chapter 5 about how to become your best self, even if you don't feel like it). Family lawyers usually have trial skills because that is the system most of us were trained to work in (the adversarial system used in family courts was inherited from the civil and criminal litigation models). We are not supposed to be friendly or accommodating. We are smart, tough, and can be brutal gladiators. Some clients seem to want the lawyer with the toughest reputation. At least that is the conventional wisdom. I'd ask you to explore that idea a bit more closely.

Are you interested in a public fight, or are you more interested in a discreet, amicable divorce where your needs will be met, where you will be heard, and where you and your spouse will show each other the dignity and respect that you each deserve? If those are you interests, then the collaborative divorce model can serve those interests well, whereas the traditional divorce model may not.

I am interested in the interplay between psychology and the law. I think that overly aggressive family lawyers have a chip on their shoulders. It is as if they really wanted to be trial lawyers in the big leagues with the civil litigators but ended up in family court because they couldn't cut it.

That may be unfair. But when we look at divorce as a grieving process, as we do in the collaborative model, it is hard to understand why smart, capable, skilled lawyers who want to help people would choose to engage in the type of adversarial warfare that we see so often and is scientifically proven to cause such harm to families and children.

I see divorce, in the collaborative model, as a personal growth opportunity for me and my client. A common and articulated goal of many people who choose the collaborative divorce model is to walk away feeling content and reasonably satisfied.

To the extent that I can help my clients find their voice and emerge healthy, stronger, and financially secure, that is what I like to do. Many collaborative attorneys share this philosophy, but not all traditional lawyers do. I suggest you ask lawyers you are interviewing about their philosophy of divorce and their approach to divorce in general. Like most things at this point in your life, it is important to use your words and be clear about your needs and what you expect from your lawyer, beyond the basic ethical requirements for lawyers to be competent, skillful, maintain confidentiality, and avoid conflicts of interests.

It is vitally important to find a lawyer you can trust and with whom you get along and, yes, even like a bit. You and your lawyer will be spending up to six months (or two years, if you ignore my advice and choose to litigate) together during the worst time of your life, where the most private, painful memories of your past will be revealed. You may be wondering, *Is that necessary? Why does the lawyer need to know these gory details? How can the past inform the present and the future?* If you are thinking that, I'd ask, "Are you serious?"

You and your spouse developed a certain dynamic during your marriage. That dynamic will be played out in your divorce process, unless you uncover it, name it, and consciously choose to develop a new way of dealing with each other. It was the nature of that dynamic that led to your divorce and current discomfort. Do you really want to continue with that pattern into your future? I think not. You have a choice, but you need to be willing to explore what the marital dynamic was and be willing to, first, take responsibility for your role and contribution to that dynamic; and, second, change it for your own well-being and the well-being of your family.

This is necessary. You may be wondering *how do I find a good lawyer?* Start by looking up collaborative divorce lawyers near me, review their website, see whether they identify themselves with the International Academy of Collaborative Professionals or have other insignia that demonstrates their commitment to this paradigm. Then you can call one and schedule an exploratory interview. This will help you understand how the collaborative divorce process works in your specific area.

If you choose to ask your friends, parents, coworkers, or just go online, it is likely you will miss the opportunity to find a collaborative divorce lawyer who aligns with your core values. This is because most of your family and friends have never heard of collaborative divorce, so how can they steer you to such an attorney? And most people you ask had horrible experiences with their own divorce or watching their parents' divorce, so they are also biased and may steer you to an overly aggressive family lawyer, out of fear, because your situation triggers old memories from their lives. If you want to see the difference between an initial intake with a collaborative attorney and a traditional divorce attorney, you can try that out as an experiment. I think you will see the difference right away.

If you choose not to engage in a collaborative divorce, then make a short list of lawyers that you can see yourself working with after you have been through their website. Discover for yourself what you think their approach and philosophy may be. Then, schedule an in-person interview, or a telephone call. Many lawyers still offer a free consultation; others don't so be prepared to pay for an initial consultation.

Just remember, you get what you pay for, so if lawyers charge for an initial consultation, do not be offended. Keep an open mind, and you will learn something new from the lawyers that you interview. Once you have your list, you may be wondering, *how will I know if I have a good lawyer?*

LISTEN AND LEARN: HOW TO INTERVIEW AN ATTORNEY

Just so you know, when you think you are interviewing me as your divorce lawyer, I am interviewing you. I do not need your case. If I do not think we will be a good fit, either because of our personalities or the subject matter, I will decline the request to represent you. Not every lawyer has that perspective or ability to say no. Some lawyers fear that they must take your case, whether or not they like you, and may not worry about being a "good fit." I think that is a bit reckless from the lawyer's point of view and will likely lead to dissatisfaction and conflict for the client as well.

If you are interviewing collaborative attorneys in your area, they will likely be part of a professional "practice group." The practice group is a unique interdisciplinary professional network of lawyers, mental health professionals, and financial neutrals. The group is formed with the common attraction to collaborative divorce as a process.

These people are all deeply committed to learning about each other, both professionally and as people. Relationships are at the core of collaborative practice. This is true not only for your relationship with your spouse, but also for the relationships between the professionals who may form the team that supports you and your spouse through the process.

Your spouse also likely will interview a collaborative attorney from the same practice group. If the lawyer you or your spouse are considering for a collaborative case is not part of a practice group, I'd ask them why not? Some lawyers may say they are "collaborative," but they have never been trained; some lawyers may not get along well with others, and perhaps they were intentionally not included in an established, functioning practice group. This should be a red flag for you.

To build a successful collaborative divorce team requires that the professionals trust each other's judgment, ethics, and knowledge in their specialized field of practice. Professionals only learn to trust one another by spending time with each other, doing trainings together, meeting on a regular basis to talk about cases and best practices, and learning about each other in a way that builds rapport.

Collaborative professionals work with other collaborative professionals that we know, like, and trust. This is good for you and your spouse, because a healthy team can model positive, non-defensive communication. The lawyers will be cooperative and non-adversarial. The teams that work well together can ease tensions and demonstrate good faith and fair dealing while moving your divorce forward in an efficient manner.

If you decide that collaborative divorce is not for you, here are other things to consider when choosing a traditional divorce lawyer: Do you want a large firm or a small one? Each has advantages. There are no right or wrong answers here.

Some larger law firms assign your case to a junior lawyer whom you did not choose. Sometimes a paralegal may be doing some of the work. You may not have been aware of these facts, and it is important to ask these questions so that you know what to expect. Much of the work of a divorce can be handled by a skillful paralegal.

When you go to a deposition (a formal procedure where you are under oath, with a court reporter and your spouse's lawyer asking you questions, in advance of trial, ostensibly to obtain information from you, while also potentially setting a trap to catch you in an inconsistency or lie to use against you in trial), or a mediation, or to court, then you want your lawyer to be with you and prepared for those big milestone events.

Because a partner's hourly rate is higher than an associate's, you should expect an associate or a paralegal to do some of the paperwork, but for a deposition or evidentiary court proceeding, you want the partner you hired to be prepared and available. Also, ask about double billing, and how the associate or paralegal will be billed. Will the lawyer also charge for "reviewing" or "revising" the work that the associate or paralegal already charged for? Most lawyers are careful not to double bill, and most are mindful about the costs of a case. Note that I said *most*. Find out which kind of lawyer you are dealing with by asking questions in your interview process.

You should find a lawyer you trust and believe will help you through this process, whichever process you choose. If you are looking for a divorce based on principles of integrity, decency, mutual respect, dignity, and transparency, then you need to honestly assess whether this lawyer's reputation in the community and your direct experience of the lawyer in the interview support that approach.

If your gut tells you that this lawyer is not for you, then don't feel any pressure to retain him or her. If you already hired the lawyer but it is not working for you, you can always fire the lawyer and find another. You can do that at any time. Obviously, if you are both in court and in an adversarial proceeding, it is rare, but it does happen more these days, that you and your spouse can choose to step out of the adversarial arena and try the collaborative divorce model. You just need to hire collaborative attorneys. If you think you need a gladiator, and that is your intention, then find the lawyer you need.

Once you have assessed the lawyer's philosophy in relation to your goals, interests, and needs, then you need to assess whether the lawyer has the skills and desire to implement the strategy to meet your needs.

Questions to consider, whether you are hiring a traditional lawyer or a collaborative lawyer:

Does the lawyer have a website that explains his or her philosophy and approach to divorce?

The Collaborative Divorce Lawyer

Collaborative divorce lawyers will be very up front about their approach to divorce. They will proudly display their affinity for the collaborative divorce model, and they will most often carry the insignia of the International Academy of Collaborative Professionals somewhere on their site. They will also promote their skills as mediators or peacemakers. They frequently spend quite a bit of time explaining the collaborative divorce model and why they like to use it.

Some collaborative lawyers will only practice collaborative divorce or mediation. Others may still offer an adversarial, in-court model for clients they think need that type of support. Read what they have to say and see if it resonates with you. If they have a link to their practice group, follow it. See who else is out there in your community and read their websites, their bios, their story. You are interviewing someone for a very important job. Do your homework!

The Traditional Divorce Lawyer

The traditional divorce lawyer's website will not mention collaborative divorce. You can still learn a lot from reviewing a lawyer's website. You will see her approach and from her bio, her years of practice. You can assess who else is in the firm: staff or other lawyers.

Make sure you read the website before you schedule an appointment so that you can do a deeper dive into their approach to divorce. Remember, just because a name comes up on the first page or two of Google doesn't necessarily mean that he is your best fit. Those are often paid advertisements. I suggest you look a little deeper than what at first appears the most visible. Read reviews and testimonials.

How do I know this attorney is a good match for me?
You will be forming a very personal and intimate relationship with your divorce lawyer. Depending on your needs, this relationship may last a few hours to a year or two. You may pay this person for a few hours of time, or thousands of dollars a month. You cannot hide from a good divorce lawyer. A good match is someone who you feel listens to you, cares about you and your family's success into the future, and someone with whom you feel safe sharing the most intense feelings (and shameful moments that we all have during marriages when, in hindsight, we did not act the way we wished we had) that naturally arise during this process.

How much will this cost?
If you think you need a lawyer, it will cost you something. Remember the adage you get what you pay for? This applies to divorce lawyers.

Of course, you might be able to get a free consultation. Some lawyers still offer free limited introductory service. Sounds good, right? But think about it. What should you realistically expect from a half-hour free consultation? I suggest that you manage your expectations. Before you meet with any lawyer, the firm will want to know your name and your spouse's name for a conflict check.

A conflict check is ethically important so that the lawyer does not end up in a situation where she has already spoken with your spouse, established some rapport, perhaps obtained some confidential information that would not otherwise be public. If that happened, and even if your spouse did not choose this lawyer, the lawyer would be disqualified from representing you. A lawyer cannot represent two people in a single matter where your interests may conflict and where the lawyer obtained confidential information in the initial intake.

People routinely think that because they hope for an "amicable divorce" that they can share a single lawyer to help save costs. We can't do this: ethics prohibit our representing a current or former client against another current or former client. We cannot represent two people with potentially conflicting interests, and two people getting divorced are viewed as classic potential for conflicting interests.

Sometimes people think that they can disqualify all the "good" lawyers in the area by making free consultation calls. That is a common adversarial tactic, but technically, an actual conflict of interest occurs only if the lawyer receives confidential information that could be used against that caller in subsequent litigation. Simply giving an overview of process options, for example, or an overview of the law of the jurisdiction, without obtaining details, does not generally create a conflict of interest.

I defeated that tactic in a case where a batterer was calling every lawyer in the northern part of the state in a specific effort to create conflicts. I was very clear on the phone that I did not represent people at that time who had restraining orders against them. I did not take any further information from him and told him that I was not available. Shortly thereafter, the wife called me. I realized the game, and I decided to represent her. The husband objected and with his new lawyer tried to get me recused. I did research and found the ethics opinions to support my continued representation. The court agreed.

However, if that is not your situation, then in the collaborative divorce community, some lawyers will invite you and your spouse to a high-level process call together. You meet the lawyer together and hear about your divorce options together. Then, if you both choose to use this process, you decide who gets to work with the initial lawyer; and the lawyer will share names of other collaborative attorneys in the practice group so you can interview them as well. Be aware that this is not common practice, but it is a growing practice. It is still more common that you and your spouse each will find a collaborative divorce lawyer and schedule your own initial meetings.

The idea of a joint initial meeting to understand the process is valuable for clients. First, it takes the sting out of the experience; as a couple, you hear the same information at the same time, so one spouse does not feel at a disadvantage in terms of information; and you and your spouse get to meet one of the lawyers who will be part of the team. This can be more comforting to know up front, rather than allowing your mind to run amok with dark imaginings about the lawyer your spouse will to choose.

If you and your spouse meet together with a single collaborative attorney for a process-only consultation, you will sign a waiver of any potential conflict of interest and agree that the information you are receiving is strictly related to the process. You will not get answers to specific, substantive questions about the details of your case. You will receive a frank and open introduction to the options you have, including collaborative divorce. Unless you live in Canada, lawyers are not required to tell you about collaborative divorce as an option. So, you can rest assured that if you find a lawyer who proudly identifies as a collaborative divorce attorney, you will hear about the other options as well (DIY, mediation, and litigation), whereas if you go to a traditional lawyer who is not trained in collaborative divorce, you may miss the collaborative divorce part of the orientation completely, because they will not tell you about it.

In a collaborative divorce intake process, you may spend an hour or more with your attorney. This is a deeper dive than a traditional divorce intake, because it involves options that need to be explained. The collaborative lawyer will be curious about you and your family, and your life, how you are handling the emotional aspects of your divorce, how you want to handle your divorce going forward, your goals, expectations for a time line, and how you think your spouse will handle the divorce process. There is quite a bit to talk about. I tend to offer a ninety-minute consultation for starters.

In a traditional divorce intake process, you may receive a half-hour free consultation. You will get basic information you could have read on your own from your state family court website or the lawyer's own website. The information will be generic: nothing too deep or specific to your situation. For that, you need to make an appointment and pay your lawyer for her time and expertise. That is how we make a living. We get paid by the hour—the tenth of an hour, to be precise.

During a longer intake process, you can get a sense of whether you like the lawyer, whether the lawyer seems competent, whether he listens, whether you feel a connection with him. If you are in a free half-hour consult and you would like to continue, you can ask the lawyer if he has more time and offer to pay him for that time. Or thank him and acknowledge that you have used your free thirty minutes and schedule an appointment where you can ask more specific questions, then decide if this is the right fit for you and your circumstances.

How can I use my attorney efficiently?
So, you decide that you want to schedule a time to meet with the lawyer. Bring your checkbook, cash, or credit card, if the lawyer accepts credit. Do not come to a meeting, spend an hour or two with your law-

yer, and when she answers all your initial questions, empathizes with your situation, gives you solid advice, and even agrees that your friend could attend the meeting just so you could have another set of ears (we understand that it is hard to process the amount of information we are conveying to you, especially if you are feeling particularly vulnerable) and then say, "Oh, shoot, I forgot my wallet."

That is not cool. It happens, but if you want to make a good first impression with your lawyer, make sure you pay for his time.

Most lawyers work on a retainer. A retainer is a set amount of money that you pay up front, and the lawyer bills against it each month. When it runs out, you have to replenish it or make an agreement with the lawyer about how she wants to handle it. The retainer agreement is the document that your lawyer should send to you explaining in detail the billing process and your attorney-client relationship. Once you retain a lawyer (sign the agreement and pay your lawyer), if she is like me, she will be thinking about your case nearly all the time: before bed; when she wakes up; driving in the car; in the shower (no kidding, inspiration often hits me in the shower . . . I'm not sure what's up with that, but it's true). Remember, I do not charge for all those times I'm thinking about you and your situation, and I'm not at the office, or I'm not actually "working" on your case. You do get free time out of your lawyer, so when the lawyer bills you for time and asks you to pay, please give him the courtesy he deserves and pay your bill if the retainer has run out.

The next section is about how to be a client your lawyer loves. There is an inverse corollary, which is how to be a client your lawyer can't stand. Really, we have a high tolerance for a lot of bs, but not paying our bill is a serious problem for most of us. . . . I'll just speak for myself.

It is an insult for me to do the work and then not be paid after I fully explained to you at the outset how expensive and time consuming our relationship would be. I always disclose this, and for the most part, I have amazing clients and very few receivables. This is how I keep my sunny disposition as I struggle through with you, support you, and guide you during your hardest time.

How can I be a client my lawyer loves?

This thought may never have occurred to you. You may ask, why do I care if my lawyer loves me, or even likes me for that matter?

You may think to yourself, *I pay my bill each month; that should be enough.* Paying your bill is necessary but not sufficient to a healthy attorney-client relationship.

As I mentioned, my theory about clients and lawyers is either you are peas in a pod and very sympatico, or you have an alter ego type of relationship. I represent all types of people, and I have enjoyed the experience most of the time. When I have not enjoyed myself, some of these things happened:

Failure to pay. The client argues about the bill or doesn't pay it in a timely manner (it is fine to point out a legitimate error—for example, an error such as a double charge for the same day, or a travel expense that was billed twice, or something that simply got missed in the stressful end-of-the-month billing process of reviewing bills before they go out to the client). I'm talking about nitpicking a bill.

If it happens once, I consider it a red flag. Twice, and I will fire the client. I do not have time for that. I am an ethical lawyer, and I do not overbill clients. If I billed it, I did it, and it was necessary to move your case forward. If you have doubts, it is OK to raise them so that you do not feel like you are being ripped off. But if you are not satisfied with the explanation the first time and are tempted to do it a second time on a separate bill, you should consider changing lawyers before the lawyer fires you.

Micromanaging. Do not try to be "helpful" by offering to write the letters for your lawyer, or being an editor or paralegal to save yourself some money. I can assure you that it will not save you money; it will only annoy your lawyer.

We understand that you are scared and that you are very good at whatever it is you do for a living every day. Chances are, you are not a divorce lawyer. If you do not trust your lawyer to work on your behalf and in your interests, or you lack faith in their ability to do so, then you have a problem, and are not a good match. There are things that you can do to be helpful, but I suggest you just let your lawyer know that you are available if he needs additional information; the lawyer will ask when necessary.

Being nonresponsive. Most clients are awesome at getting back to the lawyer quickly. Some clients like to hold onto information longer than necessary, and some won't share basic information with their own lawyer when requested. If that is happening in your attorney-client relationship, that is a red flag, and you should talk with the lawyer about the underlying issue. If the lawyer asks for something from you, it is your job to respond in a timely manner. Each time you delay, the lawyer will charge you for following up. You might fail to produce financial information (i.e., "discovery") for any number of reasons, good, bad, or otherwise.

A cost is always associated with not responding. The lawyer has a professional reputation among colleagues and the court. When you are in a collaborative divorce, you are expected to produce information in a timely and complete manner. If you are in a traditional divorce, the lawyer's reputation with the court is something the lawyer thinks about (or should). If you are late in producing documents, then you are exposing yourself to additional legal processes to compel your eventual cooperation.

If your lawyer can't produce discovery in a reasonable way, then he or she either appears to have no control over you, looks like he is trying to delay, obfuscate, or may be just negligent. Either way, this is a problem from the lawyer's perspective. If you don't care that your fees will go through the roof for unwarranted delays, then just do your lawyer a favor and give him a heads-up that you are OK with that and keep replenishing the retainer.

At some point in an adversarial process, a judge will get involved, and sanctions are possible for willful refusal to play by the rules. The sanctions usually are against the client, not the lawyer, by the way, but if the lawyer is found to be playing games in bad faith, then the lawyer may be sanctioned as well. In a collaborative divorce, we just don't have these issues. If we encounter stonewalling, we try to address it; if it happens again, then the case is not appropriate for the collaborative process, and the process will simply terminate. We are not playing around.

Takeaways: Pay your bill; don't micromanage; be responsive. If you do those three things, you should have a relatively stress-free relationship with your divorce lawyer.

In any relationship with an attorney, if you find that your lawyer is being nonresponsive or not paying attention to the details of your case, that is also a red flag, and you have a choice: Either meet with the lawyer to discuss your concerns, or obtain a couple of second opinions and then change lawyers. This time in your life is stressful enough; you do not need to be in a battle with your own lawyer.

Sometimes clients are concerned about getting out of an attorney-client relationship, but I can assure you that it happens all the time. Sometimes people are just not a good match. It is a bit like you and your spouse at this point in your life. You need to feel supported by your lawyer. That is what you are paying for, and you deserve it. I have heard that the biggest complaint clients have about their lawyers is not returning calls. If this is a problem, you need to address it head-on. If you are in the collaborative divorce, and you find that you and your lawyer are not a good match, the participation agreement allows for you to find new collaborative counsel. The team will work with you through that transition if that becomes an issue. Your divorce should not be about your divorce lawyer. In a collaborative divorce, the lawyer is a supporting actor, not the star of the show.

How do I know whether this attorney is a good match for me?

Here you will have to go with your gut. If you have read this far in the book, you will see the different types of lawyers out there, and you should be able to recognize whether the lawyers you are meeting with fit one of those archetypes. Then, just ask yourself: Do I like this person? Do I want her to represent me? Does she represent me and my values? Am I willing to pay her to do what she says she will do? Does it feel like a good fit?

I tell my clients that they should feel comfortable with me (or any lawyer they choose), because we will be spending quite a bit of time together over the next six months to a year or more, depending on the situation. Clients tell their divorce lawyers everything. I will learn more secrets about you than you ever thought you would share with anyone other than your therapist. You should be confident that I can handle your truth. Lying is not an option when it comes to lawyers and the legal system. Liars always get caught.

PUT YOUR TRUST IN YOUR LAWYER AND THE PROCESS

Now that you have taken the time and energy to research the divorce process that will work best with you, and you have chosen the attorney, it is time to let your lawyer do his job while you get on with the process of untangling yourself emotionally from your spouse.

Thoughts to Consider

Divorce can be an expensive process. It is important to do your research, because the lawyer you choose will have a significant impact on
both the cost and the tone of your divorce.

Thoughts to Let Go

I am at a loss. I can't trust anyone. I don't know where to begin.

Practical Tips

If it makes sense, use a collaborative divorce lawyer and relax a bit,
because now you know you are in good hands, and the lawyer will not
make a difficult situation even harder.

Part II

A NEW APPROACH TO DIVORCE

4

Keep the Focus on Yourself

Stop Blaming and Projecting

HOW TO BALANCE THE INTENSE EMOTIONS OF DIVORCE

Your social, political, or professional identity, your education level, your age, or your role in the marriage does not immunize you from the emotional impact of a divorce. I tell clients that divorce is 80 percent emotional, 10 percent legal, and 10 percent financial.

This is also why using an interdisciplinary team approach to divorce makes sense, because we can all recognize up front that emotions are running high, and we don't want the outcome of this divorce to be determined by your current emotional state or that of your spouse. We want you both to feel relatively neutral about each other from an emotional point of view. In other words, we want you to be psychologically ready to be divorced. Investing time with the mental health coach on a collaborative team saves you time and money. Using your own therapist will help you move toward a sense of well-being independent of your spouse. This takes time; it cannot be rushed, or forced to occur, simply because of a court deadline or an arbitrary time line.

The collaborative team can help you stay on track and move forward with tasks that can be accomplished (such as collecting and organizing financial data with the financial neutral). Progress is always being made, even if it is not at the preferred pace of the spouse who wants the divorce over quickly. If you are the spouse who wants this over yesterday, you will face less resistance (i.e., you will have a more efficient, cost-effective experience) if you allow your spouse the dignity of time to pull himself or herself together emotionally before you start tackling the logistics of what a final settlement will look like. The skillful collaborative team members all understand this, and we work together to balance both of your needs.

Apropos of the idea that your accomplishments in the real world have little to do with how you manage your personal life or divorce is one of the funniest and saddest stories of my career. A very intense, fit, well-dressed, highly educated man walked into my office one day. He cavalierly announced that he may be the smartest person I have ever met. My eyes may have literally rolled, but I doubt that he noticed. He explained to me his undergraduate and MBA degrees from Ivy League schools; how he started several successful businesses in the United States and South America; how he spoke five languages; how he was a super dad; and how his wife was awful. He confidently stated how he may be the smartest man I've ever met.

When he finally stopped talking, I looked him straight in the eye and said, "You are clearly not the smartest person I have ever met, because you are in my office on the losing end of a temporary restraining order." Apparently, he liked that direct approach and hired me to get him out of quite the marital mess. That was not a collaborative divorce.

Whether or not you realize it, most people (who are not certifiable narcissists) need help processing the myriad emotions that will assault them daily, often moment by moment, during the divorce process that has begun or is about to begin. Be prepared for it. I told you before that I will not lie to you.

Divorce sucks, but it is an opportunity for personal growth and development. It doesn't matter whether you are the person initiating the divorce or you were the one blindsided; whether or not you had the affair; whether you move out, stay in the home, or the home gets sold. It doesn't matter whether you are a doctor, lawyer, business owner, teacher, carpenter, nurse, or stay-at-home parent. Your professional identity and education level do not immunize you from the emotional impact of a divorce.

Many emotions come out fast and furious at the beginning of a divorce—jealousy, contempt, fear, anxiety, hatred, resentment, bitterness, anger, sadness, depression. These feelings are not easily brushed aside. I do not recommend trying to short-circuit their careful analysis through excessive drinking, drugging, partying, or a new "relationship." To the contrary. I submit that having a healthy therapeutic relationship with a skilled mental health practitioner as you embark upon this very serious and necessary step toward divorce is the absolute first step out of grief and toward sanity.

Remember, this is an opportunity. You may not have asked for it directly, but it is yours now. You may be questioning what you possibly can do with all your heartbreak, grief, and fear. You can use those feelings to fuel your recovery from the effects of an unsatisfying marriage. You can take the time to grieve your losses, take care of yourself, and to find out who you really are, not who you thought you were. Brace yourself: divorce is a humbling experience, if you do it right.

It is easy to delude yourself into thinking you had nothing to do with the fact that your spouse is telling you it is time to divorce. It is a classic trick of the shocked mind to go to blame and projection. People tend to project because they have a trait or desire that is too difficult to acknowledge. Rather than confronting it, they cast it onto someone else. This functions to preserve their self-esteem, making difficult emotions more tolerable. It is easier to attack or witness wrongdoing in another person than confront that possibility in one's own behavior. How a person acts toward the target of projection might reflect how he really feels about himself.[1]

I see a lot of blame shifting in divorce. Clients routinely accuse their spouse of all sorts of things. It seems to me that the accusing spouse most likely suffers from the affliction of which he is accusing the other. Granted, it is hard to look at yourself honestly when you are being rejected in the most public way by the very person who swore an oath to love and protect you, in sickness and in health, till death do you part. This is not easy stuff.

It takes a commitment to your own mental health to do the work I am talking about, and the collaborative divorce process is designed with this commitment in mind, for both of you. It is intentionally a judgment-free zone. It takes courage to use this time when you feel like you have been punched in the gut to pull yourself up and get help. You have to get some perspective on yourself at this moment. A collaborative divorce lawyer may ask you to assess, honestly, what you may have done to contribute to this breakup. Did you cheat? Did you think about cheating? Did you patronize or otherwise assert a sense of superiority? Did you abuse your spouse, verbally or otherwise? Did you lose your identity trying to please your spouse and "save the marriage" at the cost of your soul?

Whatever it is you contributed to this mess, it is time to uncover it and own it. If you owe an apology, then rest assured, an appropriate time will come when you can apologize for your contribution. In the collaborative process, we create a safe environment for such a conversation to take place. Often, a time will come to make amends. A time will come for forgiveness. This is for you, not your spouse. It is the means to release guilt or shame. An authentic apology can set you free. You can't rush this part. Prior to that, you may feel like you are locked in a bit of hell. The good news: You have the key.

VICTIM OR VOLUNTEER?

Have you heard of the ancient wisdom that says "pain is inevitable, but suffering is optional?"

I understand this to mean that it is important to feel your feelings, and it is equally important to let them go. Don't hang on so tight to your suffering. Feel your pain, then let it go. The suffering comes when you add on additional layers of reactions and stories you tell yourself about the pain or feeling. So, for example, say you are feeling sad, or disappointed, or hurt. Rather than sitting with the discomfort of the feelings, we often try to avoid feeling bad. So, we act as if we don't feel sad, hurt, or disappointed, or we pretend that we are not feeling these things, or we tell ourselves stories about how someone else caused our feelings, or why we are justified in feeling these feelings. Many of us can't sit still with our pain long enough to let it go.

Pema Chödrön, the Buddhist nun, notes that a feeling only lasts ninety seconds.[2] When I heard that, I thought, *really? That's it?* The theory goes that if we can just sit still for ninety seconds and feel the pain or discomfort, it will pass, and we can move on without ruminating about it. What usually happens to most of us is that we feel a feeling, it feels uncomfortable, and we run. We do not want to be uncomfortable, even for a second.

In fact, when I told my daughter about this discovery, she laughed at me and casually said, "I'd give you about three," as in the number of seconds that she thought I could handle a feeling without trying to make it go away or feel better. I don't like dealing with difficult feelings any more than you do, but I try. I practice. I know it is part of my growth process as a human being. Feeling one's feelings and accurately identifying them is hard, but it's the only way through this emotional morass called divorce.

So, the trick is, just feel the pain in its most raw and unadulterated state. Do not fall for all the extra stuff such as, "I shouldn't feel this," or "Why am I feeling this way?," or "I don't have time for this." We all can afford ninety seconds to feel some legitimate feelings about the ending of what has until now been the most important relationship of our lives. Remember, feelings are not facts; they are just feelings. If we do this, the theory is that we will save countless hours of avoiding our feelings, ruminating about our feelings, stuffing our feelings, or engaging in other acts of mental gymnastics to avoid feeling them. In the long run, not feeling all of our feelings will only hurt us and take time away from living our lives.

You may wonder why a divorce lawyer is so stuck on these emotional issues. I'm trying to impress upon you that unresolved feelings cost you money with the divorce lawyer.

The choice is yours: victim or volunteer? Will you step up and take responsibility for your contribution to the problem, or not? Even if your spouse cannot own up to his or her responsibilities for the demise of the marriage, you will feel better, and be better, if you can and you do.

In a collaborative divorce, each of you will be expected to take responsibility for yourself, your feelings, and your contributions to ending the marriage. We don't tolerate finger pointing, blaming, or shaming. This is often a new experience. With the help of the mental health coach or your collaborative attorney, you will be encouraged to do the hard work of identifying your feelings and communicating them effectively.

You may also wonder why I would want to do that as part of my divorce. I'd say, for at least a couple of good reasons. First, doing so puts you in touch with your authentic nature, skills, likes and dislikes, uninfluenced by your spouse. Second, it shows you how easily you fell into an unhealthy relationship dynamic, and you want to see this clearly so you don't repeat the same mistakes with your next relationship(s). At some point, regardless of who did what to whom, you must give up your victim status, or else you start to become a volunteer for the suffering. This is not a pretty look. It is tedious to endure, and it is heartbreaking to watch.

BECOME AWARE OF THE STORIES
YOU TELL YOURSELF (AND OTHERS)

Let's talk about you first. How are you doing? Take a moment and give it an honest assessment. Before you sat down to read, what were you thinking and feeling? Are you able to focus? Scan your body, right now. See where you are holding tension. Can you tell where? If not, I'd suggest you start looking for it and get back in touch with your body.

I started seeing my Thai yoga massage therapist about a year before the separation, and continued for many years after the divorce. I loved this time to myself. My gifted body worker had noticed that I tend to move quickly through space and time, and I spend a lot of time in my head. It takes extra time for my body to catch up to my mind and for me to finally get still enough so that I can breathe deeply. I could feel my body in those moments of relaxation, and I could let go and release tension that I didn't even realize I was holding. OK, the fact that my shoulders were often up to my ears and the muscles in my neck were practically in spasm should have been a sign, but I was moving through a divorce, working full-time, had a ten-year-old child and an unruly one-year-old white German shepherd at home could have been a clue had I bothered to investigate.

It is hard to keep it all together during this time. The point I am trying to make is that you should do something physical and get back in touch with your body. Divorce is the perfect time to try something you've never done before but thought would be fun. Your body needs care and attention, because it will carry you into the next phase of your life. You deserve to focus attention on yourself and get whatever professional help you need to do so if you can.

Among the common stories I hear from clients is, "Oh, I can't go to the gym; I don't have the time or money"; or "I always wanted to paint, but I have no talent"; or "I didn't do anything to deserve" this divorce; or "everything would be fine if my ex wasn't such a jerk"; or "my ex can't have the kids, he can't cook"; or she "can't have the kids, because I'm the one who does their homework each day with them and puts them to sleep"; or my personal favorite and long-held belief, "I don't believe in divorce."

Oh, really? Well, it is about to happen, whether or not you believe in it, whether or not you asked for it, whether or not you are prepared for it. Finding the right collaboratively trained attorney and putting together a team can help you feel prepared for this major life transition. This is why I am explaining what you should expect. This is true whether you choose a collaborative divorce (which I hope you do) or something similar (also a good idea), or whether you are stuck in the old paradigm and end up in court (my sympathies are with you, but sometimes this is the way it is). You still have choices about how you handle yourself. If you find your mind returning repeatedly to an old narrative (i.e., you keep hearing yourself say the same things about your ex either in your head or out loud) and nothing is changing or getting better, then I suggest you take the time to investigate what underlying belief is being challenged, what story you are telling yourself. Then, in the privacy of your quiet space, or with your therapist, or even your new collaborative divorce lawyer or mental health coach, ask yourself whether that story is even true.

Remember, growth comes at your edge, not in your comfort zone. Push yourself a bit, accept the challenge that divorce is presenting you. Use this time to figure out who you really are, and stop putting the focus on your ex. At this point, it is not about him or her, it is about you. The time has come to debunk some of the myths and stories you have been telling yourself about why you are not good enough, smart enough, pretty enough, strong enough, rich enough, and so forth. Stop comparing yourself to anyone else, stop competing with your spouse, and stop feeling bad that you are getting divorced. It happens to the best of us.

YOU HAVE CONTROL OVER YOUR THOUGHTS AND ATTITUDES

Your beliefs become your thoughts. Your thoughts become your words. Your words become your actions. Your actions become your habits. Your habits become your values. Your values become your destiny. —Mahatma Gandhi

What does "practice" your thoughts, your words, or your actions mean? It just means you recognize and admit that you have a choice about whether your attitude will be one of empowerment and compassion, or one of victimization and persecution, for example. When you speak, are you using sarcastic, cynical, divisive language, or are your words more hopeful, kind, and understanding? What about your actions? Are you behaving in a way that comports with your values as a human being? Ask yourself whether your behavior (not your spouse's) is reflecting your best self.

You may be wondering, *Do I need to practice this stuff all the time, every day, even if I don't want to and even toward my soon-to-be ex?* My answer is, "Yes, you do." You may be thinking in that somewhat whiny voice you use sometimes when you feel a bit petulant, *Why? Why do I have to be the one to behave when my ex is such a* _____ (fill in the blank)*?*

First, your attitude, speech, and behavior are critically important because your child(ren) are watching you. How they see you handle adversity, strong emotions, massive life changes, and how you approach their other parent is what they will draw upon in their own life, now and as it emerges, for as long as they live. You are creating their "family of origin" story. Second, you need to behave in conformity with your values because you are worth it. One's self-esteem often takes a beating in a divorce, and often someone feels unworthy of love.

The opportunities to practice being your "best self" despite the madness and chaos that appears to be surrounding you are abundant in the divorce process. In the collaborative process, we sometime try to create safe-to-fail experiments, because we learn from our mistakes. Expect to make mistakes. You should not expect to be perfect at being kind to yourself or others all the time. Keep practicing. Mistakes are part of life. Those of us who find ourselves more on the perfectionist side of the spectrum need to take that lesson to heart. No one is perfect. Not you. Not me.

Have you ever heard the phrase "progress, not perfection?" Perfection is an illusion, striving for it can only set you up to fail and feel disappointed in yourself. Why do that? Practice being your best self during your divorce. When you make a mistake, you will be aware of it, and hopefully not make that one again. If you hurt someone in that process, apologize immediately. Then change your behavior. Don't do it again. Do you see how a divorce is an opportunity to practice emotional growth and maturity? At the same time, you will be teaching your children how to handle conflict, disputes, and adversity in a mature, sensible, humane manner. To paraphrase Martin Luther King Jr., "It is easy to judge a man's character when things are going well for him. It is quite another to see how he responds when adversity strikes."

HOW I KNOW THIS IS HARD TO DO

This can be a miserable and bleak time of life. However, I also believe that what you focus on comes true. What you resist persists. If you can start to focus on and seek out those people and things that bring you joy, I promise you will find yourself a few years down the road feeling joyful. You can look back at this time of your life and be proud of your own resiliency in bouncing back as well as you have from one of life's most traumatic experiences.

What I have been telling my clients for nearly thirty years has been sound and solid advice. I'm embarrassed to share that for the first twelve years of my divorce law practice, I often went to work feeling grateful that my marriage was "awesome." I was grateful that my marriage was unlike my sad, sweet clients who seemed to be struggling so much in their marriage that they were now in my office looking for help to get divorced.

I admit it now, although I am not proud of it—I felt a bit superior and insulated by naïveté. I sincerely apologize to any former client who may be reading this book (hopefully, none of you are, as I would not want to see you going through this process again, for goodness' sake). I was young and had no experience with divorce in my family of origin, and I didn't have children in my earliest days of practice. So, although my legal advice early on may have been correct, it was not informed by personal experience, for which there is no substitute.

DEVELOP A SHARED NARRATIVE

Instead of insisting on your version of reality and trying to convince your spouse and everyone around you why you are right and they are wrong, try to raise your awareness about the language you use with your children and your spouse. In the collaborative divorce model, one of the first steps we help you with is how to start a conversation right away with your spouse, either directly or through the help of a mental health professional, to create and stick to a jointly authored narrative you can use to speak with your children, friends, and family about your decision to live in separate homes.

A joint narrative can be something as simple as: "We are still a family. Your father/mother and I are getting divorced from each other, but not you. We both love you, and we believe we will be even better parents to you if we are not living in the same house. No one is to blame, and no one is at fault here. It is our decision. We are here to help you deal with this change as best as we can." Leave it at that. When they ask about details, say something like, "I understand your curiosity, but that is not a question I will answer."

Set boundaries. What you say and how and when you say it are important steps in the collaborative divorce process. It is often one of the first joint decisions you make as a divorcing couple, and you are doing it for the benefit of each other and your families. In the collaborative process, this is something to work on with the support of your team or with the mental health professional. When you have three highly skilled divorce professionals present to assist you through this process, it makes sense to take advantage of their years of experience.

Regardless of the process, it is always important to keep your adult issues away from the children, no matter how old or mature you think they are or they seem; no matter how curious they are; no matter how they attempt to manipulate your emotions. Stand strong. Stand united. It is hard. It requires that you put your money where your mouth is. This doesn't mean giving up your perspective or your voice. Sometimes that happens in a marriage: "getting on the same page" meant getting on your spouse's page. That is not what I'm talking about here. I'm talking about doing the hard work of honest communication and holding reasonable boundaries when it comes to not oversharing information with your children.

Many people in the divorce setting claim that they are acting in the "best interests" of the children. This is the modern legal standard that courts apply as if to divine some objective truth in a custody battle. People claim they are acting in the best interests of their children at the same time they justify abhorrent behaviors. Do not let yourselves fall into that trap. Do not allow yourselves to devolve to the point where you ask a judge to decide the future of your relationship with your children. Work through this. You can do it. I have confidence in you.

By keeping the focus on yourself and how you use this time for personal growth, you also allow your children to have their own experience of your ex, separate from you. Let them have their own experiences, independent of your feelings, especially these early feelings that are so raw and personal to you. They are not divorcing their parents. Do not impose or inadvertently allow your pain to seep onto your children. I know this is easier said than done, but being aware that this happens a lot is an important idea to keep in the forefront of your mind and close to your heart.

Thoughts to Consider

When you point the finger at someone else, three fingers are pointing back at you. Look at your own actions, attitudes, and behaviors. Check to confirm that you are walking the walk, not just talking the talk.

Thoughts to Let Go

I am blameless. I did nothing wrong. I did everything wrong; it's all my fault; it's all your fault.

Practical Tips

Admit you are human. You are not perfect. Own your mistakes so that you are not burdened by guilt. It is not easy to keep the focus on yourself, especially when you think you are right. Next time your spouse expresses an opinion you don't agree with, say, "You may be right." Let your spouse speak his or her mind without interruption. Be radically honest about your needs and give your spouse the dignity to have his or her thoughts and ways of being.

5

How to Be Your Best Self during Your Divorce

Working with criminal law is working with the worst of humanity.
Working with family law is working with humanity at its worst.
—Source unknown

When I first heard this quote, it was 1989. I was sitting at the bar in South Royalton, Vermont, eating french fries and having a beer with my then-husband, my best friend, my soulmate. The bartender was a classmate. He made that bold assertion, and I thought to myself, *No, that can't be right. Family law is working with humanity at its worst?*

Surely, I argued, criminals had to be worse than divorcing couples. Back then, at twenty-three years old, I had a lot of opinions, and I was clearly a bit naive about relationships and what happens when people break up. I hadn't heard of the book *Why Good People Do Bad Things*.[1]

Then I became a family lawyer. Lo and behold, I can attest to the fact that the bartender was correct. Something about the primal fight or flight response gets triggered when someone declares that the marriage is over. The "D" word is mentioned, the room starts to spin, and things go cuckoo for an undetermined length of time until the entire painful, often ugly saga has concluded. It often feels like a complete loss of control; the rejection hurts, and it can be disorienting. It is like no other pain you have ever experienced. So, expect discomfort and humility.

The question is how long you will suffer in this altered state of consciousness with cortisol pulsing through your nervous system, wreaking havoc on your sense of identity and place in the universe.

As the Buddhists are attributed to have said, pain is inevitable, but suffering is optional. This is the moment of truth. Will you let this divorce ruin you, or will you use this experience to make you stronger, wiser, more resilient? Can you rise above your circumstances and become a *better* human being? Or will you default to the lowest common denominator and succumb to becoming part of the *worst of humanity, or humanity at its worst?* The difference is but a fine one. The bar has not been set too high. You can do this. We can do this together.

Divorce may appear to be an unsolvable problem, but really it is an opportunity for each of you to find your greatest self-expression. The key is recognizing that you need each other to have a good, healthy divorce. That is the mind-set shift, the paradox, the polarity. You need to come together in order to separate.

COMMON EXPERIENCES BROKEN DOWN BY YEARS OF MARRIAGE

Let's talk about some common experiences and see if you identify with any of them. I'll break this down into classic archetypes that I have seen over the years. Every person is different, of course. I understand that you may feel different from other people you know who have gotten divorced. I suggest that you remember your common humanity here and let go of your former ideas about how unique you think you are, because the truth is you are getting divorced—just like half of the other marriages. A lawyer caveat: Please remember, I'm not talking about abusive relationships here—just regular, imperfect people trying to navigate their way out of a marriage.

See where you might be on the continuum and, hopefully, you won't feel so alone or ashamed. Divorce happens to the best of us. Getting a divorce is not a personal moral failure; having an ugly, spiteful, zero-sum game divorce is.

Families come in as many configurations today as there are people. The following categories are not meant to exclude anyone or to pigeonhole you. Some short-term marriages might be more complex; some folks have longer-term marriages where the children are still young; some people are getting married later, and some are having children but others are not. More people are in "gray divorces," in their retirement years, and these divorces have unique issues, including the emotional impact on adult children.[2] Second- and third-marriage divorces sometimes have blended families to consider.

Regardless of your situation, you are not alone. If you and your spouse know that you want to divorce well, then you should each talk with a collaborative divorce attorney so that you can obtain the support and guidance that everyone needs in a divorce, except perhaps the short-term marriage without children. At first blush, these folks may not seem to have much to argue about, but divorce is still a loss, and the couple may wish to preserve relationships with extended family and friends. Even a short-term marriage without children could benefit from the structure and support that the collaborative divorce model could create for them.

SHORT-TERM MARRIAGE: 0–5 YEARS, NO CHILDREN

We all make mistakes. True, we live in a culture of comparison and competition. We all feel some pressure to marry, but in some ways, this marriage was a misstep in your life's trajectory. There is no shame in figuring out how to promptly get out of this marriage with the least amount of drama and expense possible. I still suggest individual therapy to analyze the circumstances in your own personality that allowed you to say "yes" in the first place. It is important not to blow off this part of the experience. You may want to spend some time looking at what that was all about, so you don't doom yourself to repeat the same pattern in your next relationship.

In a short-term marriage without children, there really is no sense in pointing the finger too much at your spouse, no matter what she or he did or didn't do. Look within. Consider the upside of this divorce: You clearly dodged a bullet. You are getting out before any irreparable harm was done. Let it go.

In a short-term marriage with no children, it is common to feel initial shame and basic stupidity that you didn't realize your spouse was someone you really did not know, understand, or like. True, someone (or many people) may have spent a lot of money on a wedding, but in the end, hopefully you can look back and consider that it was a good party, even if the marriage didn't work out. Remember, at this point only your pride is wounded. You both can and will heal from the decision to divorce. It is much better that you do so now, rather than after having a child or two. Many people think that if they have a child or two it will save a marriage in distress. In my experience, that rarely works out well.

In terms of your divorce process, it helps to be kind to each other, have a chuckle at your mutual naïveté, and divide your stuff in a way that allows you both some dignity. Be prepared to leave this marriage with basically what you brought into it. This could be a classic kitchen table divorce. Divide the wedding gifts, personal property, and money you accumulated during the marriage and fill out the forms available to you online through your own state's judiciary website. If you want to use a mediator, that would be an excellent option. If you want to run your paperwork by a family law attorney, just to make sure you didn't forget anything, that is also a great idea. If the emotions are in check and the finances are not complicated, you might not need the extra support offered in a collaborative divorce.

However, if you want the support of a collaborative team, you might find the process to be useful and informative. You would have the guidance of your own lawyers. You might want to consider bringing in a financial neutral, or that might feel like overkill. You could use the process and the benefit of the neutral mental health coach to identify your goals and help you process emotionally the loss that even a short marriage represents to you. By using the collaborative process, the lawyers will take care of the paperwork for you, you and your spouse can have honest conversations about dividing assets and liabilities (even pets), and you can use this process to become more effective communicators.

As part of a closing ritual, you might want to consider doing something to memorialize the end of the marriage. Maybe send a thank-you card to your in-laws, create a common narrative that you understand everyone's confusion and disappointment, and you wish everyone a great life. It will be a great life, just without your current spouse or your in-laws in it. You always have the choice of remaining friendly. Remember, this was just a mistake. Everyone makes them. What you learn from your mistakes matters most.

SHORT-TERM MARRIAGE: 0–5 YEARS, WITH CHILDREN

Well, I am sorry this is happening to you, and it is still better to get out sooner rather than later. This situation often happens to people who thought that having children would save the relationship, or who had children by accident. At the risk of stating the obvious, having an unplanned child rarely helps, and choosing to have children because you think it will help an already faltering marriage rarely does. Having a child, or two, will not save a marriage in trouble. It just makes the divorce that much harder and more complicated. The good news is that now that you have children, and you have realized that the marriage is not working for one or both of you, you have choices to make—whether or not you want this divorce. I tell clients in this situation, "Let's play the hand we were dealt and work with what we have."

In this scenario, I am assuming that your children are still young and this is not a blended family, or a second marriage with older children. That dynamic is beyond the scope of this book, but I would encourage you to carefully consider all of the relationships that have been created and how your adult divorce may adversely impact your children's relationship with their stepparent and stepsiblings. So, let's assume young children and a short marriage. In a situation where you are sleep deprived and stressed about how hard it is to take care of another human being who has absolutely no control over his or her bowels, vocal cords, or emotions, plus the pressure of trying to spend time together as a couple, and work outside the home, I'd say it is a miracle that more marriages don't fall apart after the first child or two. Parenting is hard, whether you stay together or get divorced.

In terms of getting divorced, you and your spouse are now both required to step up and into your new role as a "co-parent." You may think you don't want to do that with the person whom you married in front of your friends, family, and the god of your understanding who now tells you that he or she wants to call it quits. It rarely looks like both of you wake up on the same day, and over coffee mutually declare your marriage over, and ask each other, earnestly, "How shall we successfully co-parent our children?"

Rather, it looks more like two people who found themselves together at a time of life when biology was calling—or two people who found themselves together just before biology was calling—or two people who found themselves drawn together by work or friends or partying. It was all fun and interesting and awesome until a baby arrived, and you had to bring the baby home from the hospital and adjust your lives accordingly.

It looks like two tired people trying to adjust to the awesome responsibility that no one and no book can prepare you for—how to raise an infant human being. It looks like a lot of bickering over small details or parenting styles; it looks like a breakdown in communication; it often sounds like one person's perception that he or she is "doing everything" while the other person "does nothing."

It looks like someone (or both people) working outside the home to make enough money to support the family and then coming home to be the "on-duty" parent. It looks like the unbearable stress of short parental leave; a wait list for safe and affordable day care; the agony of leaving a baby or toddler at day care screaming for you not to leave (even though everyone assures you not to worry, it will stop a few minutes after you leave, which is true, but doesn't make you feel better). It is letting someone else hold, feed, put down for a nap, and take care of your child while you go back to work, full of guilt about whether you are making the "right decision."

It feels nearly impossible to concentrate at work because you are interrupted by biology to "pump" like a cow so that you provide your child breast milk because you are trying be perfect and "do it all." It looks like utter frustration and a lack of appreciation when you come home from a full day at the office or job only to be greeted with, "Here, take it" (i.e., a smelly, crying, inconsolable infant) because the stay-at-home parent is at his or her wits' end from a day at home without any adult conversation. You do so lovingly because you want to be helpful, but it is never enough.

Can you see how these mutual resentments start to creep in? I'm suggesting that if left unattended, these resentments will build into a divorce. This is a divorce that divorce lawyers and the courts consider a "short-term marriage with children."

If you have a blended family, or older children who recently have had to adjust to a new marriage, home, and stepsiblings, these can be complicated relationships to untangle.

This is an opportunity to use the collaborative divorce model to help you manage, express, and let go of your mutual resentments so you and your children can have a healthy, loving, and supportive relationship with two parents and stepparents, who often provide love, and security to children, even if only for a few years. These relationships are all important. How you manage your divorce will have a direct effect on you and your children. You want that impact to be positive. The children don't need to know what went wrong between you two, even if there were serious common problems, such as post-partum depression; no sex; late nights out; late nights walking around a house with a fussy baby; overwork; lack of sleep; not enough money; or an affair (emotional or otherwise).

If your children are little, they won't remember much of these early years so long as you continue to meet their basic needs for connection, love, food, hygiene, and medical care and avoid yelling at your spouse in front of them. They will likely emerge unscathed. If they are older, you can expect them to experience your divorce as another loss. This is important to manage well, because divorce can be an adverse risk factor for children.

You have an opportunity to be happy, mutually respectful co-parents. If a spouse suddenly realizes that parenting is not really for him or her, then make healthy decisions about what roles you will play in the children's lives. In a collaborative divorce, you can be honest. There is no shame in being honest. If you don't see yourself as a fifty-fifty shared parent, then say so. If you both realize that you really love and want to care for your children, and you have both the ability and disposition (not just one or the other) to meet their current and future emotional and developmental needs, acknowledge it, celebrate it, and be grateful for it. Not everyone has that. Working directly with the mental health coach in a collaborative team can help you identify these important issues and talk about them openly and honestly. The lawyers don't have to be part of this conversation. The important thing is that you are having the conversation, and it is part of the divorce process.

So, count your blessings, because being a single parent stinks. Work through a parenting plan with a mental health coach who understands the developmental needs of children and understands both of you. People need help creating a parenting plan that makes sense. It is also important to appreciate that your spouse wants to parent (if that's true) and is competent to manage parenting responsibilities, even if he or she needs support, accommodations, or freedom to parent differently than you.

If the issue is that you can't stand how the other parent parents, then this needs to be discussed and carefully managed. There is obviously a continuum to consider. People are allowed to parent differently. No one has a monopoly on best parenting practices. All of us were raised in different environments and with different values and priorities. Having different parenting styles in most cases does not lead to children who will be psychologically damaged, become juvenile delinquents, or engage in risky behaviors.

However, if a parent is abusive (physically, emotionally, or sexually), then there needs to be a factual basis for this claim. If there is physical or sexual abuse, the courts should know about it, and restraining orders can be obtained. If there are allegations of chronic emotional abuse, that needs to be investigated as well, although social services and the courts are slow to recognize and prioritize emotional abuse, even though the impact is as substantial as physical or sexual abuse. These types of cases will likely not be suitable collaborative divorce cases.

If one parent accuses the other of abuse (physical, emotional, or sexual), then authorities charged with investigating such complaints must make a full and appropriate investigation. Some cases of intense high-conflict domestic violence result in unjustified parental gatekeeping or alienation. This is a form of domestic violence, and it causes tremendous damage to children's future emotional growth and development. Abuse, gatekeeping, and alienation are beyond the scope of this book. If you have these types of concerns, it is important that you obtain appropriate counsel and treat the matter with the utmost care and urgency.

It is well documented that fighting over children in a custody fight, putting down the other parent's parenting style, undermining the other parent, engaging in emotionally abusive language toward the children (or the other parent, in front of the children) as well as other forms of physical, emotional, or sexual abuse, unjustified gatekeeping, or parental alienation are risk factors for children. It is not the divorce itself that is the risk factor, but how the child experiences his or her parents' divorce and how the parents treat the child during the divorce process that matter most.

Please remember that. Fighting over the children causes them to be stressed and psychologically pulled asunder. It is not whether they eat pizza more than once a week, or how much screen time they have with the other parent, or the fact that they watched a PG- or R-rated movie before their time.

By using a collaborative divorce model, you can use this time to create reasonable boundaries and standards over basic parenting such as bedtime routines being similar at each house; nap times during the day; food allergies or the introduction of new foods; sharing a notebook or log that travels with the child so that parents know what milestones may have happened during the other parent's time, or what medications or illnesses the child may have. If you use a day-care provider, then I suggest that you purchase three of the exact same calendars so your child can become familiar with the schedule of contact and who is picking up the child and when. You can use a parenting app to keep track of the calendar for events.

If you have older children who are showing signs of stress, depression, or anxiety, then you two must recognize that your attitudes about each other may be a very large contributing factor to your child's stress. You need to come together, find a good therapist, and make the effort to put your children's best interests ahead of your own feelings. This is much easier said than done.

It is important that children have roughly comparable standards of living at both homes, so you will need to address any gross disparity in incomes. You do this, in part, because it is important that your children do not perceive the disparity in wealth in a way that naturally leads them to want to spend more time with the wealthier parent. Sometimes, a child perceives a wealthy parent as having more authority and power in the relationship. You can each have different values about money, but the children should have roughly comparable standards of living at both homes so that you demonstrate to your children that you want them to feel safe and secure and loved in both homes.

If you don't know how to have this conversation with your spouse in a healthy way, this is a good time to start post-separation communication coaching with a skilled mental health professional. If you choose a collaborative divorce model, you can expect these types of supportive, although difficult, conversations. By using a mental health neutral in a collaborative divorce, you are not attending "couple's counseling" to get back together. You are using the neutral coach to learn more effective communication tools so that you can use your words and express your feelings, frustrations, and appreciation in a safe environment.

Divorce at its best allows you to feel empowered to speak your truth so that you do not vibe your spouse with hostile, passive-aggressive nonverbal communication. That communication style effectively undermines the character of your spouse in front of the children. They can sense it. It also demonstrates to them that you haven't successfully worked through your emotions. Just because it is a short marriage doesn't mean the feelings of loss are not substantial, for either you or your spouse.

The general rule about property division in a short-term marriage is leave with what you brought into the marriage. If there is a gross disparity in wealth, there probably was a prenuptial agreement that likely will be enforced. Generally, prenups are enforceable when there was full disclosure of assets, income, and liabilities; each of you had a lawyer; the agreement was reasonable and fair at the time it was signed, and it is still reasonable and fair to enforce it at the time of a final divorce. If there was no prenup, then any claims for spousal support (alimony) will be met with a skeptical eye in a short-term marriage.

However, even with a prenuptial agreement, if your spouse needs short-term financial support, above and beyond child support, then it might be an option to discuss and consider. Your collaborative attorney can help you understand and negotiate these types of issues as part of your divorce. If you are not in a collaborative process, then these are the types of issues that you should consult with an attorney to understand your options and help you negotiate. This could be at the kitchen table or mediation or as part of a traditional divorce process.

MID-TERM MARRIAGE: 5–10 YEARS, NO CHILDREN

Feeling like a failure is a common experience, regardless of how long you stayed married. However, if your marriage has ended in fewer than ten years, it is likely that you will be upset. I usually see conflicts over money or the lack of children. One person may have said he or she was "open" to the idea of having children down the road but, in truth, never wanted them. Or someone's biological clock has kicked into high gear, and what you thought you both wanted when you set out on this journey simply turns out not to be true. This situation represents a real loss of what you thought you would have in your future, regardless of gender.

In the mid-term marriage, often around year seven, someone may have an affair. Many people say that the affair was "just emotional, not physical." I usually don't believe that, but even if true, it still represents a betrayal. It is hard to recover a sense of respect or trust for the spouse who has left the marriage.

Even though children won't be part of the divorce discussion, other important relationships have developed during a marriage of this duration. There are important relationships with in-laws (mothers, fathers, sisters, brothers); friends you developed as a couple; friends that each of you brought into the marriage; colleagues and other members of the community that you will see and eventually tell that you're getting divorced.

How will you handle this? Will you at least try to create a common narrative for why you are breaking up, or does everyone and anyone who will listen need to hear about what a louse your spouse is for treating you so badly? Will you portray yourself as the victim of this decision or step up and work through a sensible plan to untangle your marriage so that you can grieve your losses and move on?

Depending on your roles during the marriage and any disparity in your incomes, you should expect to discuss how to divide your marital estate and whether one of you needs additional support to get back on your feet and establish a new, separate household and life.

Because the idea of spousal support (alimony, or spousal maintenance) is such a drag for so many reasons for both of you, perhaps it makes sense to consider a disproportionate property settlement in lieu of alimony. This way the break is clean, and no additional feelings of resentment are created by the monthly obligation to either write a check to your ex or wait for a support check from your ex. Remember, alimony is modifiable in the event of a substantial change in circumstance, so you might end up back in court if something significant happens to justify changing the alimony amount or duration. Property settlements are final and not modifiable. The pros and cons should be discussed with your attorney.

A divorce in a marriage of fewer than ten years, without children, can be a blessing in disguise. It allows you to look back and say either:

"I really did love you there for a time. I just don't feel that way anymore";

or

"This basically sucked for the last number of years, and thankfully, we can end it in a way that works for both of us."

You can divide your personal property and settle the finances, stay friendly and not shame and blame each other. You can wish each other well as you move on to the next stage of your life. I consider this a no-harm, no foul divorce. There is often no reason to be hateful, stingy, or mean-spirited.

In the collaborative model, you can have a simple, peaceful divorce and maintain your friendship if you want. Often, one or both of you just need time to realize that it will be better for both of you to get out of the marriage sooner rather than after you have had children. Consider yourselves lucky. If you do your inner work, you have every opportunity to emerge from that first marriage healthy, openhearted, and wiser for your next relationship. This is especially true if you have taken the time to work through the legal, emotional, and financial aspects of the divorce using the collaborative divorce model. Or if you feel like fighting about it, you can go to court and probably spend as much or more with adversarial lawyers and end up with a similar outcome as if you had chosen a more peaceful, thoughtful approach. The choice is yours.

MID-TERM MARRIAGE: 5–10 YEARS, WITH CHILDREN

Read the part about short-term marriages first. That is how you got here. Read the bit about short-term divorces without children as a general reference for how to divide your property and for ideas about income equality. Now add child support to the settlement discussions. Child support is driven by a guideline in most states based on your respective gross incomes, with some additional factors, such as the cost of health insurance, extraordinary medical or educational expenses, additional dependents, and qualified day-care costs.

If you are curious what the child support amount might look like, Google child support guidelines for your state and see what pops up. It should give you a basic starting point. But, alas, although that may be interesting, it is not really the point of this discussion.

If your children are older, they will be impacted by your divorce in a much more conscious way. They can now express themselves. They have a ton of needs that you still must meet (consistency, stability, emotional and physical safety, friends, homework, sports, music, and more). They may have simple or profound questions about why this is happening.

You need a common narrative. Remember, they did not ask for this. As parents, you are demanding that they adjust to a new reality they did not ask for, at the same time you both are adjusting to a new reality, whether or not you asked for it. I urge you to be gentle and compassionate with yourselves so you don't screw this up.

If you are the spouse asking for the divorce, put yourself in your spouse's shoes and be mindful about not pushing or moving this divorce along too quickly. If you are the spouse receiving the news and feel "blindsided," then I suggest you need to get to therapy, *pronto*. Your denial will not help the situation. Whether or not you realize it now, your marriage is not falling apart solely because of the acts or omissions of the other. That may sound harsh, but it is true. If you are not the spouse who stepped out of the marriage, had an affair, or for unknown reasons wants to call it quits, I do empathize. I'm not condoning what your spouse has done, nor am I judging you. I'm just saying that it takes two to tango.

A marital dynamic is at play in a mid-term divorce with children. If you don't know what I am talking about, it might be worth exploring this question with a skillful marriage counselor—not with the goal of reconciliation, although that can happen, but rather with the goal of determining the nature of your dynamic. This is good information and awareness to bring into a collaborative divorce case. If you don't understand the dynamic, you are likely to be subject to its unconscious influence throughout your divorce process. Sometimes by seeing it and naming it, you can move beyond it.

I find it helpful to reframe the divorce to a simple this marriage is not working for you as a couple. Society foists the label of a "failed marriage" upon us. Just because your marriage didn't work out does not mean you are a failure or that you will fail at parenting your children. You need to separate those two ideas. It is very hard to do, given the dominant paradigm of divorce in our culture that seeks to affix blame. Separating yourself from the dominant paradigm is especially hard to do in the first few days, weeks, or months after your spouse tells you that he or she wants a divorce.

You may notice that everyone around you has an opinion about divorce. Unless they are divorce lawyers, and preferably trained professionals in collaborative divorce, I suggest you take suggestions from family and friends with the grain of proverbial salt. Seriously, do not take legal divorce advice from someone who is not a lawyer. And if the lawyer's first instinct is to sign you up, obtain a retainer, and file your divorce paperwork in court, then I'd suggest you obtain a second opinion from a specially trained collaborative divorce lawyer in your community.

In my experience, mid-term divorces with children are some of the hardest to understand and manage, because one spouse usually does not see it coming. These divorces usually happen when there is an affair, or where addiction or untreated mental health issues arise and there is no space or ability to communicate openly and honestly about how you *feel*. Feelings get stuffed, and resentments build, until there is not much is left to say. Communication fails.

This is where the troubles you may have noticed (but ignored) from the short-term marriage were allowed to grow and fester without appropriate interventions. Although neither of you is happy, one of you may have thought, *Oh, well, I'm sure this is the way it is for everyone. We are really busy with the children; and my spouse (or both of us) is really busy with his/her career; sure, we haven't had sex in god knows how long, and we are like ships passing in the night, but isn't every marriage like that?*

I have no idea. I can't answer that question. I see you when you or your spouse have decided that this is not the way to live, and someone wants a divorce. Usually, both of you are stunned by this admission, but the person who finally musters the courage to say it out loud probably has been thinking about it for much longer than the spouse receiving the news. It happens all the time.

If you are the driving force for the divorce, and you suspect your spouse really has no clue about how unhappy and disconnected you feel, then when you announce that you want a divorce, you should expect your spouse to feel shocked, betrayed, and upset. That is not the best time to file for a divorce. The best time to file for a divorce, says the divorce lawyer, is when you both are *psychologically ready* to get divorced. The time is when your shocked spouse is no longer shocked; when his or her grief has moved from anger to sadness to acceptance, not still pissed-off and feeling betrayed. All of this transformation can take place within the safety and structure of a collaborative divorce. You get the benefit of moving the divorce forward while taking time to address the emotional aspects before trying to tackle the financial or parenting logistics.

The best time to get divorced is after you have allowed your spouse sufficient time to realize for himself or herself that getting divorced is in both of your interests and in the long-term best interests of your children and the family. This may take some time, but it is worth the patience. It will save you money and it will spare your children, friends, and family from bearing witness to a vengeful, spiteful, ugly divorce. It is easy to anticipate strong negative reactions to feeling rejected. I'm not talking a lot of time, but seriously, given the length of your marriage, is it too much to give your spouse and parent of your children a month or two to process the news that will change their life forever? I'm not saying you won't get divorced; of course, you will. I'm just saying that you have an opportunity to do this thoughtfully. The collaborative team can help you both put together a plan of action and execute it with compassion.

By now, do you see how all these intense emotions make getting divorced not just a simple legal procedure? Engaging in a divorce process with someone who is not psychologically ready to admit that it is really for the best is likely to be a divorce based on negative unresolved emotion instead of logic and love.

Yes, I just used the word "love" in relation to divorce. As Tina Turner sang, "What's love got to do with it?" To which I reply, "A lot."

I think it is important to admit that at some point in the past ten years, you loved your spouse. I remind you now, so you can remember that you were the one who declared your fidelity, loyalty, and love in a public ceremony with witnesses because you thought it was the right thing to do. Feelings clearly can change over time, but it often seems easier to try to erase your past love, companionship, and the good times you did have with a broad-brush stroke. Resist that temptation.

In my initial interview with clients, and sometimes throughout the case, I hear complaints about the other person. I frequently ask my clients who are complaining, "Why did you choose to have children with this person if they are so awful?" It is fine to change your mind about not wanting to stay married, but it is not OK to deny that you loved your spouse. I'd even argue that you still do love your spouse (on some level), but you want to live separate and apart. Love and divorce are not mutually exclusive. Again, that is the paradigm shift I'm talking about. You have the capacity to hold both of those concepts at once in your mind. Try it.

You are reading this because you want peace in your future, and you do not want to screw up your children. All the psycho-legal literature acknowledges that the worst thing for children is to have their parents fighting about them or around them. They do not want to take sides. They love you both. They need you both to develop a healthy self-consciousness, to feel *whole*. With all that in mind, can you now see how this mid-term marriage with children will take a little more effort, a little more patience and intention, than a divorce without children?

At this point, it doesn't really matter what you or your spouse (or the in-laws) did or didn't do. You two are the parents of children, regardless of their age, or stepchildren you love. You need to start acting like you care about their well-being.

It is easy to talk the talk; it is hard to walk the walk. Shall I explain what I mean? It means that at the beginning of a separation, with minor children, many people think it is "in the best interests of the children" to spend all their time with "me" and to have limited time with the other parent. This applies to stepparents as well. I'm just saying, this is the wrong mind-set to start a healthy, happy divorce and post-divorce life. Divorce with children creates a minefield for potential conflict, which with some degree of grace and dignity, you can learn to manage.

I understand you may be hurt, vulnerable, confused, and have a host of other feelings, but work with me here. I'm just the divorce lawyer, not the mental health professional. I care about your feelings, and I understand that they exist. I'm just not the professional who can help with that aspect of your divorce. That is why I told you in chapter 1 to find a good mental health professional for yourself and why I recommend the supportive interdisciplinary team of a collaborative divorce.

It is now chapter 5. If you haven't found yourself a good therapist yet, what are you waiting for? It won't get better for you until you give yourself the gift of time and space to identify and then release your emotions and come to better understand and appreciate yourself and your spouse. It is hard to have a decent divorce, let alone a good one, if you both cannot see the value in personal therapy or at least some therapeutic help to unpack the marital dynamic that contributed to the breakup.

The most successful post-divorce parents are the ones who have insight into their own contribution to the end of the marriage. These parents also understand how hard it is to put the needs of the children ahead of their feelings, and they seek out appropriate professional support.

I know the idea of post-separation counseling is weird, but in my experience, couples who do this together find it helpful to successfully navigate the complexity of a divorce with children, whether or not they are minors. What am I talking about? Counseling with your ex? Yes. Call it "divorce coaching" or "post-divorce communication coaching." Just don't call it "marriage counseling," because reconciliation is not on the table. Further, if you use that term, the therapist you find to work with you as a couple may erroneously think that you are trying to salvage the marriage. If you are not sure whether to divorce, a therapeutic process known as "discernment counseling" might be something to consider. Learning to communicate effectively so that you can parent your children is the purpose of this exercise. This type of work during the collaborative process creates a safe space to talk about the weekly happenings for the children, how you are each processing the emotions of the divorce, and generally help you both navigate through the complex terrain of raising healthy, resilient children in our modern culture with all its potential and challenges. You do this "off-line" from the team, because your lawyers don't need to be present for routine but important conversations. The collaborative lawyers want you to have a place and person to continue to work with you both after the collaborative process has ended. If you start your working relationship during the divorce process, this counselor can continue to work with you after the divorce. It may not feel like it now, but you will thank me when a situation arises with your children regardless of their age, and you have the other parent to lean on in times of trouble or crisis.

LONG-TERM MARRIAGE: 15–20+ YEARS, WITHOUT CHILDREN

At first blush, this seems like it should be an easy situation to resolve. No children. What is there to fight about? Well, by now I hope you realize that even if you don't intend to "fight" about anything, this archetype still suffers the same pain and grief as any other marriage. And, if you are not careful, you will find plenty to "fight" about.

For instance, I have the dubious honor of taking the first (and currently only) dog custody case to my state supreme court. I still think we should have won that one. Although it is undeniably true that people and their animals are deeply bonded emotionally, the courts still view domestic pets as property, and property gets divided. No room to share a pet in our jurisprudence, absent an agreement to do so.[3]

We invest our hearts, souls, and money in long-term marriages. A lot can happen in fifteen or twenty-plus years with someone. Careers are built, homes are made, relationships with extended family are deepened (or hardened), networks of mutual friends are developed, and a lot of married people without children have the same issues, just not the child element. Folks without children also may have well-established roles in the lives of their friends and families who have children, such as being an aunt, uncle, godparent, or less formally as confidant or trusted friend.

A divorce has the potential for couples to lose all that same sense of identity and belonging that has been created over the past fifteen years or more as in any other divorce. So really, it is not "easy" or "simple" just to say, "There are no children." It is a myth to think, well, they don't have kids, what is there to fight about?

Let's start there.

Say you value your spouse as a person, but you have just come to terms that the marriage isn't working. Say you tried marital counseling and have concluded that you don't want to be miserable for the next 20–30 years of your life. You can get divorced. Just remember that your spouse probably won't see this coming. You could argue that counseling should have been a tip-off, but sometimes denial runs deep. Even if you have talked about "problems" in the marriage (with or without professional assistance), someone will *feel* blindsided and betrayed. Just recognize that up front and be prepared to work with that. All of the previous advice applies to you, too.

If your spouse is still an important person to you, if you would like to part as friends without bitterness and resentment, if you want to preserve relationships with the community and extended family that has become yours, too, during the marriage, then getting divorced still will require insight and skill to do it well. This is a good time to consult with a collaboratively trained divorce lawyer.

What do I mean by insight? I mean taking time to become aware of how your behavior contributed to the breakdown of the relationship. Learn to take responsibility for your actions. Accept your role. Say you are sorry for your contribution to ending the marriage. Accept what is happening. With insight, you can both then find skillful lawyers, preferably collaboratively trained ones, to talk about how to divide your marital estate; talk about alimony; create a common narrative for your friends, family, and community; and divorce with dignity and mutual respect for the time you spent together. You might also want to consider a good-bye conversation, where you can take time to write a parting message to honor your past and what you appreciated and learned from your spouse during your marriage.

Of course, you could also choose to ignore me and spend the next year or two paying lawyers to get your "day in court" to explain to an overworked judicial officer why your spouse is such a louse and why you deserve 10 percent more than the last offer that was made. That is always an option. Did I mention that for every hour of court time, it takes about seven hours of preparation time? Do the math.

LONG-TERM MARRIAGE: 15–20+ YEARS, WITH CHILDREN, MINORS OR ADULTS

All right, friends. If you are in this group, I'd say you are in good company, and the most common demographic in my practice. There are many reasons why after all this time you or your spouse may be calling it quits, done, over, or "just not working anymore." If you both agree that the marriage isn't working, then that is a good place to start, and it might make the experience a little less painful. It is still a loss, and a grieving process, even when you know it is the right thing to do.

Maybe you've exhausted all your options. You've tried counseling and simply concluded in an honest, up-front mature manner that you want the other to be happy and you want to be happy, too.

Truth is, you both deserve to be with someone who can love you the way you want to be loved at this stage of your life. What you wanted when you were twenty-five or thirty-five may not be what you want when you are forty-five or older. It doesn't matter the reason for the divorce. When you both know it is time, you can still divorce with dignity and mutual respect.

Depending on the ages of your children, you will still want to be mindful of the narrative you tell them. It is easy to mistakenly assume that just because the children are no longer minors that your divorce will not have significant impact on them. In fact, research suggests that the impact on adult children of divorce is significant. It is different than the impact on minor children. Adult children may worry about the parent they deem more vulnerable. They may be worried about the financial impact on their lives; they may be stunned to find out that the happy home life they thought they lived was a mirage; they may worry that they will end up divorced; or they may worry about where they will go for the holidays, or how the grandchildren will be impacted. The considerations are myriad. I've heard of plenty of adult children who refuse to speak to a parent because of the way the divorce was mishandled. There is a great book about the impact of divorce on adult children, *Home Will Never Be the Same Again* by Carol R. Hughes and Bruce R. Fredenburg.[4] I highly recommend a deep dive into this topic if this situation applies to you.

Let's assume for a moment that you are not exactly the model of emotional maturity I've described above. Let's say that your spouse has been having an affair while you have been working like mad to pay for the college tuition and to plan for retirement, and your feelings seem stuck in a loop that ranges from rage to excruciating betrayal, loss, and sadness.

Let's say that your spouse has developed an addiction to pills, alcohol, or pot, and you have tried every co-dependent coping strategy you can possibly think of to get him or her to stop. You feel like you are walking on eggshells, nothing you do is ever right or good enough, and your self-esteem is basically gone. You are exhausted, depleted, and sad. Or let's say that your spouse is a workaholic, and you've been feeling a bit depressed yourself because you get zero attention and haven't had sex in years.

Or your spouse has become distant for some reason you can't explain, and it feels like you are two ships passing in the night now that the children have moved out. Nothing is wrong that either of you can explain. It is just something you feel—like the distance that creeps into many marriages when you realize that you don't have much in common anymore, especially if child rearing is completed, and you now have an "empty nest," and you just don't want to share the rest of your life with the same person.

No two divorces are ever alike, but they have common themes as we discussed in the earlier archetypes. The longer the marriage, the longer it may take for you to recover/rediscover who you are at this point in your life and who you want to become in your post-divorce life.

Ask yourself now, "What do *I* want?" When was the last time anyone asked you that? Ask yourself, "How do *I* want to show up for this divorce and the next stage of *my* life? Will I allow this marriage and divorce to define me for the rest of my life? Will I feel heartbroken, betrayed, bitter, and resentful because all my early dreams for my future with my spouse are being destroyed by one word, divorce?"

You can choose that path. That is an option. I'd urge you to consider an alternative narrative, which sounds something like, OK, true, my ideas about how I thought my marriage and life would turn out were not accurate. I have some mixed feelings about all of it. I think I might need a therapist to sort through how I am feeling. On the one hand, I'm sad and feel regret that it didn't work out; on the other hand, I'm kind of excited to think about my options. I like the idea of exploring things that I like to do; it might be nice to live in a home without having to compromise constantly, and do I really want to live in a home with someone who doesn't want to be with me anymore?

Here is something you may not know: Although men may initiate a divorce and are likely to receive more money and be more financially secure than a woman after the divorce, women are happier in the long term.[5] If a woman initiates the divorce, you can bet she will be happier about this decision than any other she has made thus far in her life. The decision to divorce is both the best decision for some, and the hardest. Regardless of gender identity, divorce generates strong feelings, and it is a complex exercise.

It is time to build your emotional intelligence muscles so you can handle it. This may take a little time. I'd argue that you are not in a rush, which is another good reason to choose the collaborative process. With help and guidance, you will move through the various stages of grief; at the same time, the team is holding you both accountable to do the legwork of gathering financial information and planning for your future. You won't be rushed to a decision, but you will have all the elements organized for the time when you say, "OK. I'm ready to do this."

Sometimes a spouse is in a rush, because he or she is "in love" with someone else. Yes, I am rolling my eyes. I am not a fan of my clients telling me to hurry up the divorce because they "finally" found the "one" who loves them like their spouse didn't. I tell these clients that it took fifteen, twenty, thirty years to get into this financial and/or emotional mess, and it may take time to get out of it. Divorce is not a rush job. You should expect at least six months before the emotions settle down to the point where a serious conversation about options can take place. It just takes that long. Sometimes, it takes even longer.

Let's assume you just told your spouse in a long-term marriage that you want a divorce. Your announcement is coming to your spouse out of left field from her or his perspective. I'd urge patience and empathy to start. Then, add a dash of generosity, and I'd say you can have yourself a very decent divorce in a 6- to 8-month time frame. Be discreet and honor all the years you spent together with your spouse, building a family, being part of a community. It wasn't all bad. Stop acting like it was. There is no need to have a bitter, angry divorce; if you rush an unprepared spouse through the court process, that is likely to be the result, and likely backfire.

Long-term marriages with children are the quintessential archetype for going to court to play out a drama of hurt feelings and unsatisfied dreams. Resist the temptation. The money you save in attorneys' fees could be used for the kids' college education or your first vacation alone, a retreat, or other serious self-care opportunity to heal from the pain of a divorce and find your best self—the person you were destined to become, not the version of yourself from twenty years ago, or even who you've come to expect of yourself. Divorce can be the catalyst for you to reconsider your current attachment to your identity.

Collaborative divorce presents an opportunity for transformational, personal growth and change. How to do this is covered in chapter 6.

Thoughts to Consider

Understand your personality type, your conflict management style, and how the marital dynamic established during the marriage will likely impact your divorce process. Ask for help so you can stop repeating unhealthy patterns.

Thoughts to Let Go

You are unique. No one has ever gone through what you are going through. You cannot handle this. You are embarrassed or ashamed that your marriage didn't work out. You will lose people in your life you care about because they will inevitably take sides.

Practical Tips

Take time for self-care and reflection. Keep the focus on yourself, not your spouse.

6

Let's Get Down to Collaborative Business

CREATING THE TEAM: YOUR COLLABORATIVE ATTORNEY

Let's say you and your spouse have done your homework. You have decided that you would like the assistance of the team approach, and you have found your collaborative attorneys. You should expect to receive an intake form and a retainer agreement from your lawyer, explaining how you will be charged for the lawyer's time and expenses. Many attorneys still require a retainer. A retainer is an advance against which the lawyer can bill and be paid for future work.

When the work is performed, the lawyer is entitled to bill and collect payment from the client trust account. The retainer is money that is deposited into a special lawyer trust account, called an IOLTA account. It stands for interest on lawyer trust account. These accounts are regulated by the bar association in your state. Lawyers have special ethical requirements to keep your money in trust, not co-mingle it with their regular operating expense accounts. You should receive a bill every month from your lawyer that details the work done on your case. Your lawyer pays himself or herself from the IOLTA account and sends you the bill and an accounting of the amount left in your retainer account after that month's work was billed.

It is typical to replenish the retainer account as the case moves forward. It is important to talk with your lawyer about his or her billing methods and expectations. If you ever have questions about your bill with a lawyer, it is imperative that you speak up and share your concerns. Getting divorced is an expense.

Soon after retaining a lawyer, you will also receive a draft participation agreement. This is to read on your own and then review with your attorney *before* you sign it, so that you understand and fully consent to the collaborative process. You may also receive a road map or some other documents that your collaborative team will use to keep track of where you are in this process.[1] Every collaborative divorce has roughly four stages: initial preparation, information gathering, idea generation, and document production and signing.

Your attorney is there to answer all your questions and offer legal and other guidance throughout the process. You may have a lot of questions when the process starts. I think it is reasonable to schedule a call, even a short one, once a week or once every two weeks at the beginning to check in with your lawyer. You are entering a new process and meeting new professionals you are supposed to trust. I find it takes a little time to establish trust with people. This usually happens after a couple of substantive conversations.

I encourage you to write down a list of questions as they pop into your head. When you get three to five questions, send an e-mail to your lawyer or schedule a call. Lawyers usually charge by the tenth of an hour, or sometimes by the quarter of an hour. If I can answer multiple questions in the same 6 minutes of time, you get more bang for your buck. If you choose to send an e-mail to your lawyer each time you have a question, it will get expensive very fast.

In my experience, each of your collaborative attorneys will speak with each other directly and will put together the rest of the team in anticipation of our first full team meeting. The lawyers will recommend the mental health coach(es) and a financial neutral. If for any reason you or your spouse don't feel comfortable with the initial intake with either neutral, speak up. Sometimes the fit is not quite right. We can make an adjustment. More than one adjustment per professional category will likely be seen as a red flag by the team, because it will appear that one of you cannot get along with others. If that is true, the team will have to assess whether you two are a good fit for the model.

MEETING THE MENTAL HEALTH COACH

You and your spouse will schedule an initial intake with the mental health coach and the financial neutral. These intakes may look different. You will sign separate retainer agreements with these neutrals and pay their deposit directly to them. You both will be responsible to ensure that their bills are paid in a timely manner.

In the single coach model, you may meet separately depending on the preference of the neutral, or you may meet together with the coach so that you can each experience the coach for the first time as a neutral, and the coach can experience you two together and see how your dynamic unfolds. It is not a judgment; it's data that is important for all of us. Couples have a dynamic.[2]

Whatever the dynamic was that you established during the marriage, it is likely to appear in the divorce process. If we need to make changes in the way you two interact and communicate with one another, it is good to see early in our process how you two communicate.

Sometimes, the coach prefers to do a deeper dive to better understand your family of origin story; and any issues of trauma, mental health, or complex family dynamics around parenting or money. Even though you presumably have heard all of that before, sometimes people feel more secure speaking freely in a private session, without their spouse present. Either way, the mental health coach is a neutral and should present as professional and unbiased.

In the two-coach model, you will meet with your designated coach and establish your relationship for the duration of the process. When you each have your own coach, it does add a level of complexity and the potential for additional team dynamics, but it also gives each of you a designated person who is with you throughout the process, helping you in whatever ways you may need. The coaches speak with each other, and they can bridge misunderstandings while demonstrating and facilitating new positive communication strategies that can serve you both for years to come.

Each model has benefits and costs. Your collaborative attorney will explain to you the custom in your location. Either way, the coaches are essential to success and cost management. They are often viewed as a comfort to most couples going through the divorce process. Their job is to normalize intense emotions and create safe spaces for each of you to articulate your feelings. By dealing with the emotions first and foremost, they help move our process forward. They are not here to judge you or make mental health diagnoses.

Remember, these folks are highly skilled at relational dynamics and have extensive clinical experience with all types of issues. It is unlikely that whatever you and your spouse are doing is new to them. They often have their finger on the pulse of the underlying emotional triggers that divorce will undoubtedly bring up for you and your spouse. We want to know about these triggers in advance, so we don't inadvertently activate them. Collaborative divorce is a trust and accountability building process.

MEETING THE FINANCIAL NEUTRAL

The financial neutral is often a critical member of the team. These folks love helping people understand their financial realities, and they seem to enjoy what they do. The financial neutral will schedule time to meet with you for a short initial intake to answer any questions you might have about his or her role. They will talk with you both about your financial resources and your respective comfort levels discussing and managing money. They will create a checklist of important and relevant documents so that there can be full compliance with your state's financial disclosure requirements for a divorce. The collaborative financial neutral is often highly skilled in conflict management and understands that people have a lot of feelings when it comes to their money, or their perception of what is their money.

The financial neutral will be the point person to collect, organize, and present the financial data to the lawyers and to each other when we get there. They will not sell you products or manage your money. They will help generate ideas that make sense when the time comes for settlement discussions.

PROFESSIONALS DEBRIEF TO ASSESS SUITABILITY OF CASE

The professionals will schedule a meeting as soon as possible after you have met with the coach and the financial neutral. At this meeting, the team is starting to establish relationships with the other professionals, especially if we haven't all worked together before. In some locations, where collaborative divorce is already becoming more popular, some team members may have worked together before while others have not. Having prior experience can be a benefit, because the team members know they can trust their colleagues. Building trust and accountability is important not only for you and your spouse but also for the professionals so that your experience of the collaborative process is a positive one.

The coaches will share their impressions and information with the attorneys; this is an opportunity for your spouse's lawyer to start to understand you, and for your lawyer to learn more about your spouse. This is useful information sharing so that your lawyer can help you manage yourself and your expectations of your spouse during the divorce process, and vice versa.

Assuming no red flags to proceeding appear, the professionals will schedule our best dates for our first full team meeting and prepare a simple agenda for it. Most meetings in the collaborative process are two hours long. We find this is a reasonable amount of time to discuss substantive issues without overloading one's senses. The first meeting as a team to get your divorce started can be an emotional experience. It becomes real when we come together to meet and talk about your intentions for your divorce. We know you are nervous and want to get started.

FIRST FULL TEAM MEETING

The first meeting is intended to be an icebreaker. It is designed to introduce the lawyers to the spouses and discuss what to expect from our process. We will not resolve your divorce in this first meeting. If there are "pressing concerns," we will identify them in advance of the meeting and put them on the agenda for discussion. These issues may or may not be resolved that day, but we will acknowledge that they exist and plot a strategy for the most cost-effective way to manage the issues that you or your spouse have raised.

We view this first meeting as an opportunity to go over the collaborative process and to make sure that everyone has signed the participation agreement. This is the glue that binds us together. We will ask you to share briefly why you chose this process and what you hope to gain from using it. The lawyers will introduce themselves to you in an effort to humanize ourselves and show you that we are here to help, not to make your life miserable.

This is a very different experience from the way most folks get a face-to-face introduction to their spouse's divorce lawyer. In a traditional case, the first introduction to your spouse's lawyer might be an initial letter you receive from your lawyer that seems to be describing a person you do not recognize. It often includes some of your worst attributes or most recent mistakes, with the added bonus of some formal financial discovery. The first in-person meeting might be a deposition about financial matters, or the day of a court proceeding. You would never be allowed to speak directly to your spouse's lawyer, and vice versa, without permission of your lawyer, who is unlikely to grant permission in an adversarial context.

What are typical "pressing concerns" that might show up on an agenda for the first meeting? These would include issues such as cash flow, separating accounts, housing, "nesting,"[3] what to tell the children and friends and family, or what kind of parenting schedule might work. The concerns can be any number of issues that may be unique to your family, including medical issues, vacations, new partners, scheduling challenges, or any other issue that seems to need a decision in a relatively short period of time.

Depending on the issue, we can discuss which professional would be best to handle the conversation and how much you might be able to resolve on your own. We can set our next meeting dates so that we can stay in touch with each other and make sure we are making progress. We would set out homework assignments and realistic deadlines for financial disclosures to the financial neutral. We would share with you any other issues that we know you will have to deal with that might be unique to your local jurisdiction and practice.

That's it. We've just started your divorce. No service of process by a sheriff; no nasty lawyer letters; no demands for financial discovery— just a gathering of professionals to help you strategically plan for a peaceful and amicable divorce.

MEETINGS WITH YOUR COACH

We have found that the more you and your spouse use the coach during this process, the quicker you will work through the inevitably painful feelings that accompany every divorce. The sooner you work through the pain, the sooner you will reach a final agreement. We have found that folks who want to skip this part of the process usually regret it. So do the professionals. Attempts to avoid the hard emotional parts only delay the way in which the emotions will show up in our negotiation process down the road. The emotions always show up. It is how you manage them that is most important, and managing them early saves time and money.

It can be useful and productive to meet with the coach together when you are working on your joint narrative to your friends and family. Because most of your friends, family, neighbors, and colleagues may not know about the collaborative divorce process, you can practice what you want to say. You can practice asking for support from loved ones, even if they think you are nuts, or have other judgments about you, your spouse, and the process you want to choose to divorce.

I suggest that you not take divorce advice from anyone who is not a professional with collaborative training or a divorce lawyer. This includes your spouse and parents. You and your spouse can work with the coach about parenting schedules and the intense emotions that are triggered when you start to think about your identity as a parent, or you can explore a nesting plan, or anything else you think they can help you with so that you can start to feel OK about your decision to separate. You will want to think about your divorce narrative and plan and practice what to say to the children, and when. The team can help with this; we have seen many iterations of this done well, as well as botched efforts. Telling your children is an important moment in their lives. You want to be exceptionally mindful about the words you choose and the vibe you and your spouse create when you tell them. This takes forethought. I don't recommend doing this one spontaneously or on the fly.

Throughout the process, you are always welcome to meet with the coach separately if you are having a particularly tough time with the divorce, or something your spouse is doing that is annoying you for which you want support. You can also invite your attorney to such a private meeting, if you and/or the coach think that would be helpful to move the process forward. It is expected that you will have your own outside therapist because the coach is not your individual therapist. It is a subtle but clear distinction. For example, the collaborative coach is not bound by the same confidentiality rules that your therapist is bound.

We also support the use of an adjunct divorce coach who could serve as a family therapist after the divorce process has concluded. Then you have established a therapeutic relationship with a professional who can help you both through the day-to-day challenges of getting divorced and coparenting the children.

MEETING WITH THE FINANCIAL NEUTRAL

Much of the work with the financial neutral can be done remotely. That person will set up a secure link for you to easily share confidential documents, such as tax returns, retirement statements, banking, credit card, and investment accounts. The lawyers usually have access to this data as well, as we like to keep track of what is coming and going.

We expect that one of you has a greater interest and ease with the family finances. We expect that one of you may need extra support to can gain confidence when it comes to understanding the financial impact of this divorce, how to create a budget, let alone live on one, and what the divorce means for your retirement. This is entirely normal.

Regardless of what else your spouse may have done, if you can trust that your spouse will share financial data honestly, then you are probably good candidates for collaborative divorce. If you seriously doubt that your spouse can be honest, think you are being defrauded as we speak, or have a legitimate reason to believe that your spouse is hiding assets and will lie, then you should discuss your concerns about using the collaborative process with your attorney. Over the years, I've noticed that many people fear that their spouse may try to hide information, but having a spouse who is doing so is not as common as one might expect. If your spouse is truly hiding assets, this will be a problem in your divorce, regardless of which process you choose. Even in litigation, finding hidden assets is not easy. You should expect to spend a small fortune to hire expert forensic accountants and engage in expensive financial discovery, which may or may not yield the full disclosure you are entitled to, especially if your spouse is as skillful as you suspect.

Let's assume you have a basic level of trust in the integrity of your spouse. Now we can talk about what to expect next when it comes to finances and division of assets, liabilities, and incomes.

We expect you to work directly with the financial neutral and be responsive to that person's request for information. The quicker you respond, the quicker you get divorced. If the neutral needs to involve lawyers because the the neutral is having trouble gaining your trust or compliance, then this will increase the costs.

The lawyers will nudge you to gather and send financial documents they have requested. Remember, each time the lawyers get involved, the cost of the process increases. To the extent that you and your spouse work directly with the financial neutral, your lawyer doesn't need to be involved, and you are saving money and moving forward, together. When you or your spouse follows up with a request for information, you are building trust and accountability. These are good qualities to develop in your divorce process.

Once the financial neutral feels satisfied that all the relevant data has been gathered, or at least enough to make preliminary observations, the neutral will put together a spreadsheet or two. The neutral is not here to tell you how to divide your marital estate. Ultimately, that decision will be up to you with the input of your attorney. Through discussions a desirable resolution will be reached and hopefully everyone feels psychologically satisfied with the final settlement.

Until then, the financial neutral will share the data with the full team so that we are all on the same page. Sometimes this information can feel overwhelming, so if that happens, separate meetings can be scheduled for you and the financial neutral and your lawyer. Whether you want the coach there is up to you. Most folks find that the support of their attorney and the financial neutral is enough, but money is an emotional topic. If you know you are likely to have strong reactions to the financial conversations, it behooves you to get the support you need.

OTHER NECESSARY PROFESSIONALS

Often other professionals may be necessary to help put this whole new life together. For example, we may need an appraiser to value real estate; or a realtor to do a market analysis, or to help find alternative housing, or to possibly sell a marital home if that is the ultimate outcome. If a small (or large) business is involved, we will want a fair assessment of value, and a business appraisal may be necessary. If there is a pension or other deferred compensation plan, we might want an actuarial analysis of the present value of the asset.

In the collaborative model, the lawyers will recommend a professional that they each trust will provide accurate data upon which we can all rely. There will not be a "battle of the experts," as there is in traditional litigation. A battle of the experts happens when you cannot agree on the valuation of an asset, and you each hire an expert to appraise the property.

In a traditional divorce, the appraisals may be so far apart as to be useless for settlement purposes. Sometimes they are close enough to reach a stipulation as to value, and then the lawyers may be able to settle the case. But if the experts are too far apart in their assessment of value, they become the focus of a court hearing. A judge's job is to listen to the evidence and decide which expert the court deems more reliable. Often unimpressed with either expert, the judge may pick a number somewhere in between, which is within the court's discretion. Sometimes, a judge may be impressed with your spouse's expert and disregard your expert. That is an unsatisfying and expensive experience. I can assure you, after you have spent thousands (or tens of thousands) of dollars on an expert, you want the judge to believe that person.

So, we don't do that in a collaborative divorce. We find someone the team trusts will be reasonable and the best fit for the issue. If one of you doesn't agree with the analysis, we can get a second opinion. Sometimes the expert doesn't get it right, or one of you can't believe that this is the reality. A second opinion can help. Our process is designed to be responsive to your needs. Everything is negotiable, except your values, of course. Don't compromise on those. No one in a collaborative team would want you to compromise your values, but we may ask you to stretch a bit where you can.

THE GOALS MEETING—SECOND FULL TEAM MEETING

The greater danger for most of us isn't that our aim is too high and we miss it, but that it is too low and we reach it. —Michelangelo

Setting goals for yourself during a divorce helps ease the pain and focuses your intentions on you and your well-being, which is exactly where your focus needs to be right now. We live in a culture of pleasing people. Many of us were raised with the false idea that our priority should be to take care of others, that taking care of ourselves first is selfish.

Thinking, writing, and then sharing your goals for this divorce is crucial to your successful achievement of them. Even if you can't achieve them all, taking the time to identify them and share them is an uplifting and positive first step forward.

Whichever process you choose: mediation, collaborative divorce, or even the adversarial path (I know, you didn't want that path, but if your spouse either chose it intentionally, or didn't understand that there were other options, or you didn't have the ability to persuade him or her otherwise), you still can use this divorce as an opportunity to set your intentions for yourself and your family. Aim high. Your experience of this divorce is unique to you, and you have every right—I'd argue, a duty—to set goals for yourself now, so that when your future arrives, you are not surprised by it or endlessly blame your divorce for the fact that you are unhappy.

In a collaborative divorce, we value the process of setting goals. We share literature with you about how to set goals. The "goals meeting" is literally the first substantive meeting we have as a team. These goals will help motivate you to get up each day; they will improve your attitude and mental health and increase your performance in other areas of your life, both personal and professional.

How long has it been since your spouse asked what you truly wanted from life? More important, how long has it been since you asked yourself? You are on the threshold of an entirely new stage of life and personal growth and development.

When starting this exercise, it may be tempting to simply write down all the things you think you want out of this divorce: sole custody; a certain dollar amount of support, or the house, as examples. It is common for one person to feel entitled to everything.

This happens when the couple has not had enough time to slow down and process all the intense emotions surrounding the divorce itself. Feeling entitled and wanting revenge are common attitudes and appear to be an initial reaction to the idea of divorce for many people. One person feels entitled to everything because he or she did not "ask for this divorce." Another may want to give it all away in an effort to assuage guilt, remorse, or as a desperate attempt to run as fast as possible to the end of the process to avoid the pain that the decision to divorce is presenting to oneself and one's family.

We cannot run away from our pain, and we cannot continue to act as if this divorce is a one-way street. If it is not working for one of you, then it is not working for both of you. That is OK. You can still get divorced and be friends and effective co-parents. Because the divorce process will take effort, why not take the time at the outset of this massive life transition to identify your values, goals, and conflict style so you can create a plan to emerge from your divorce healthy and wholehearted? This is the beginning of the paradigm shift.

In a somewhat ironic twist of fate, divorce provides the perfect platform to discover who you are at this time of your life and to seriously question and identify how you will walk through and live your post-divorce life.

Remember, your lawyer is trained to solve problems. Lawyers are constantly canvassing the landscape for a solution to meet the interests of our clients. All too often, while we are focused on the destination, the resolution, the "win," many of us miss the opportunities for healing and growth along the way.

We fixate on the outcome, as opposed to the process. This is where the collaborative practice model shines a bright light on the opportunities for empowerment and camaraderie. It starts with setting goals. The goals help focus the lawyers and the team. It helps the divorcing couple with their complex emotional history to normalize that it is OK to start thinking about an independent future.

There is a difference between a goal or interest and a position. In the collaborative divorce model, we avoid positions and focus on goals, interests, cares, or things that really matter to you.

The "goals" meeting is one of the first things we do as a full team. Our experience has been that sharing goals at a meeting is a satisfying experience. It starts by taking time to think about and write down what you really want for yourself and your future. Your goals are personal to you and are not dependent on what your spouse thinks about them. We create a safe environment to share your thoughts. Your lawyer will want to review your goals before you share them with the group, to make sure that you haven't inadvertently slipped into positional statements.

A simple example of the difference between a position and a goal would be something like: I want alimony. I want the marital home. I want sole custody. Those are all positions.

Can you imagine for a moment how your spouse is likely to respond to that? "I don't want to pay alimony. I want the marital home. I want sole custody."

Now where are you in the negotiation process? Impasse, right out of the gate. Conflict, right out of the gate. Positional language says, I am rigidly fixed and inflexible.

What if you said, instead, "I'd like to live in a comfortable home in the same school district as the children's school. I'd like to have sufficient income to support myself and be able to take a vacation like we did during the marriage. I want to spend as much time as possible with the children while they are still at the age where they want to hang out with me. I'd like to get the divorce done as soon as possible because my lease ends in three months, and I want to buy a home so I don't have to move twice."

Do you see the difference? The latter statements are concepts that the team can work with and are unlikely to be seen by your spouse as controversial. When you have taken time to consider your goals, the collaborative team can help you achieve them because we understand the underlying motivation. We can talk about solutions that work for you, your spouse, and your family. We can be more creative. And, because we have spent time building trust, we have the ability to work out temporary agreements that, for example, would allow a spouse to purchase a new home while the divorce is pending, instead of waiting for the divorce to be final, or worrying that doing so would put you at a disadvantage if your spouse later changed positions.

Goals can be short term, medium term, or long term. They can be about finances, the emotional impact on the children or family, parenting issues, personal growth opportunities, or ideas that you have secretly wanted to pursue but knew that your spouse wouldn't support. Now is your time. These are your goals, and they are independent of your spouse. If you want to spend half the year abroad, then say so. If you want to start a small business, then say so. If you want to quit your job because you hate it, then say so.

Setting goals is a transformative process. By putting time and energy into your vision of yourself in a few years, you are able to look over the horizon a bit. And by writing it down and saying it out loud to the team, you create the conditions by which your dreams have a better chance of becoming reality.

Another surprising thing happens when you share your goals in a collaborative team meeting: You find that you and your spouse share many of the same goals. This is encouraging. It is one of the first exercises where you can see that even though you are getting divorced, you and your spouse still have a lot in common. It is also an opportunity to acknowledge that your spouse has different dreams than you do, and this is an opportunity to wish that person well in his or her endeavors.

ADDITIONAL MEETINGS AS NEEDED

At this point, you may or may not be still living in the same house; you may or may not have told your friends and family; you may or may not have told your children, minor or adult; you might be considering "nesting," in which minor children live in the marital home, and the spouses take turns leaving the house so that a parent can be alone with the children in the house. Sometimes it is nice to have some peace in the house, especially if tensions are getting high. Nesting requires good communication and trust. Sometimes people share an apartment as the place to go when they are not with the children in the home; sometimes each person gets his own space or can spend time with friends or family. This gets old after four to six months, but it can be an effective stop-gap measure. Nesting is something to discuss with your spouse, coach, lawyer, or the team.

From the time of the goals meeting until your final meeting, you will go through quite the transformative metamorphosis, if you are willing to change. This is where your personal therapist or private divorce coach can come in very handy. Unpack your resistance to change. Understand what benefit you still gain by holding onto your old narrative or beliefs. Allow yourself the opportunity to grow and become the best version of yourself. This is what happens in a collaborative divorce process, because you do not have to spend three to six months focused on how to prepare for court hearings or otherwise engage in the repetitive patterns of unsatisfying communications with your spouse that led to the divorce in the first place. This is not easy work, but it is satisfying if you take it seriously and show up for the conversation.

PUTTING IT ALL TOGETHER

However long it takes (three, six, eight months or a year or two), a time will come when you and your spouse agree to wrap this up. That is when you are both psychologically ready to be divorced. This happens naturally in every case— a magic moment when you both realize that this is the best for all involved, and you no longer feel that acutely negative charge around your spouse. You may feel a bit neutral toward your spouse or pretty good even. You can see how life will be fine, if not better, without being married to your spouse anymore. You see that your children are doing well wherever they are in their own process and experience of your divorce. You've managed to improve your communication. The last challenging hurdle for your collaborative divorce team is to help you put it all together. There may be some last difficult conversations when it comes to the final settlement terms, but you will negotiate this with your lawyer's help, encouraged to make as many reasonable accommodations as needed to get this done. The lawyers are not about to let all this hard work fall apart. We are all motivated to make the final settlement decisions. Once made, the lawyers will share responsibilities for drafting all the different documents that you will need. Each state is a bit different. The lawyers usually check in with each other, review each other's work, and correct any errors or omissions. Collaborative lawyers in a collaborative divorce do not take advantage of each other's mistakes. We fix them. When the lawyers and other team members are satisfied with the final products, we will send them to you for final review and consideration.

You and your spouse will each have ample opportunity to review all the documents on your own, and with your lawyer or any other support person. If you have questions or changes, we can discuss them and see if your spouse agrees. Eventually, the agreements are as good as you will get, and both of you will need to apply a dose of good faith and flexibility, even to the best drafted document. Life can get messy, and your divorce documents may or may not address what is coming down the road for you and your former spouse to manage. What is important to remember is that you now have the confidence, ability, and support to work through anything.

Once you and your spouse and the lawyers sign the documents, the lawyers will file them with the court. Your lawyers will explain your local process and what to expect in terms of receiving the final divorce decree. In the collaborative process, we like to offer at least a short, final good-bye conversation. You might be sick of the whole process at this point, but saying good-bye to your spouse in a ceremonial way is good closure.

Divorcing well is probably the toughest experience you will ever tackle. And tackle it you did, with strong work and support.

Thoughts to Consider

Do I want an amicable divorce? Do I think my spouse would want an amicable divorce? Am I willing to ask for a different type of divorce process? Am I afraid to stand up to pressure from friends or family about how I should divorce? Is having a future, functioning relationship with my former spouse important to me?

Thoughts to Let Go

Collaborative divorce sounds weird. I don't know anyone who has done this before. I'm scared to try something new, even if it might help me and my family.

Practical Tips

Find a collaboratively trained attorney in your area. Look for their affiliation with the International Academy of Collaborative professionals. Research collaborative divorce attorneys or a collaborative divorce practice group of professionals near you. Read websites to find a professional to guide you. Schedule an introductory meeting, with or without your spouse. Tell your spouse that this is what you are doing, and you hope you can have a truly collaborative divorce.

7

The Power of an Authentic Apology at the Right Time

> If done correctly, an apology can heal humiliation and foster reconciliation and forgiveness. A genuine apology given and then accepted is one of the most profound interactions between civilized people. —Beverly Engle

About five years after my divorce, when I was still not speaking to my former spouse, we found ourselves at a legal conference in the same room where the presenters were talking about apologies and the law. It is rare that the words "apology" and "law" are used in the same sentence. The irony of that moment was not lost on me. We smiled awkwardly at each other and said nothing. I was deeply uncomfortable for ninety minutes.

By the end of the presentation, I was sure he would have learned something of value, and I honestly thought he would apologize to me. Alas, he didn't. Clearly, my evolution was not exactly progressing either, because I did not choose to rise above my hurt feelings to even see my contributions to the divorce at that time, let alone ready to offer an apology. Opportunity missed.

I don't want you to miss an opportunity to apologize for whatever role, big or small, you had in the demise of your marriage. An appropriate moment will likely organically present itself during your divorce process, or you may need to create an opportunity. Regardless of the timing, organic or planned, you must be able to apologize authentically. Do not do it if you can't be sincere. An insincere apology is not worth the effort and may prolong the animosity between you.

THE POSSIBILITY FOR EMOTIONAL CLOSURE

In the collaborative divorce process, we want to provide you with some sort of emotional closure. It doesn't have to be a formal apology. It could be a simple moment of appreciation. It might come at the end of your divorce process when you have had time to reflect on some of the better attributes of your spouse and the life you had built together up to that point. You could appreciate his or her willingness to participate in the collaborative process, or appreciate some other contribution that person made to your life. I would caution against expecting an apology from your spouse, either spontaneously or in return for your kind words of appreciation or apology. As noted above, expecting your spouse to apologize to you may be the epitome of setting yourself up for disappointment.

In the Netherlands, lawyers practice the collaborative divorce model, too. They introduced a specific process in their non-adversarial divorce, or collaborative mediations, called the "good-bye conversation."[1]

In that exercise, each spouse is given the space to clearly articulate the real reasons underlying the divorce. This is considered a "paradoxical intervention," because at the time you and your spouse are generally at the lowest point of your communication abilities, this conversation requires that you be precise in enunciating the reasons and underlying feelings that led to the decision to divorce. This can be a useful exercise, because often the spouse who did not make the decision to divorce doesn't really understand why this is happening. That spouse may start to generate "false beliefs, misunderstandings, incorrect assumptions, and wrong attributions of intentions."[2] Correcting this misinformation is important for healing. This can happen earlier in the collaborative process, or even in a mediation with a skillful mediator, or as I have seen it practiced, at the end of the collaborative process.

Some people want a closing ritual of some sort; some don't. Either way is OK. Just be sure to ask for what you need. If you think it would do your soul good to share closing thoughts with your spouse, then ask for the time to do so. This can be done after the settlement documents have been signed and filed. It should be about yourself, what you have learned and what you appreciated about your spouse over the years, or even most recently. There are no rules. Speak from the heart and focus on yourself. Do not use this opportunity as your final attempt to shame or blame your spouse. Those days need to be over.

AN AUTHENTIC APOLOGY IS A GIFT

The moment an authentic apology is offered in a divorce, it is a gift. If you are giving it, then it is an opportunity to unburden yourself from guilt, which could cripple you for the rest of your life. If you are on the receiving end of a legitimate, heartfelt apology from your spouse, this is a moment of grace, an opportunity for forgiveness. This radical act of courage will set you both free. It is a profound moment. I suggest you keep your eyes open and seize the moment when it arrives. If you get to the end of your divorce process, especially a collaborative divorce, and you have not had an opportunity to express your regrets for the demise of the marriage or causing your spouse harm, then you should speak up and ask to create that moment. Like everything in life, timing is very important. I've seen an appropriately timed apology shift the mood in a negotiation and settle cases. If the moment doesn't naturally present itself during the negotiation process, I'd suggest that you prepare a short, concise statement for after you have signed all the paperwork. This way, your words won't be misconstrued as trying to manipulate an outcome to your advantage. You literally have nothing to lose at this point by being honest.

I'm not saying you must identify everything you ever did that was wrong or hurtful. But I am suggesting a thoughtful, insightful overview of your contribution to the problems in your marriage that led to divorce. This is a healthy exercise. I suggest that you start to think about this early in your process, so that by the end you have something sincere to say. It doesn't have to be a masterpiece of oratory. A simple acknowledgment that you are not blameless and that you are sorry for any harm you have caused will suffice and be well worth the effort.

This would also be an appropriate time to acknowledge something positive about your spouse and your marriage as you look back on it in its entirety. When you remember some of the positive aspects of your marriage at the time of the divorce, it helps you both feel better, like you are not failures just because you are getting divorced. Remember that divorce narrative we talked about earlier? This apology and acknowledgment of your spouse is how you will be better friends and co-parents.

Think about it: This will be the last time you will have this level of intimacy and an opportunity for vulnerability and connection as a married couple. Don't blow it.

WHY AN AUTHENTIC APOLOGY WORKS

That law and apology course that my former spouse and I sat through was presented by a team of medical malpractice experts. They reviewed the social science literature that concluded when a doctor makes a mistake, even if the patient dies, an authentic apology reduces medical malpractice suits. The idea presented was that when a doctor demonstrates humility and compassion toward the family, admits the error, and takes responsibility for the mistake, the family is less likely to sue the doctor or the hospital, and the cases can settle out of court. It is when traditional adversarial notions of denying liability, circling the wagons, casting blame on others (including the victim), or when other forms of deflection are used in serious situations, when people are hurt or killed, that people feel even more wronged, enraged, and then sue the doctor and the hospital. This results in expensive litigation and delayed healing from the grief and loss. Do you see the parallel to your divorce?

Studies and books have been written about the power of apologies, how to do them effectively, and the psychological benefits to the person apologizing as well as the person receiving the apology. The benefits to a sincere apology are rooted in the psychological needs we have as humans to be seen, heard, and acknowledged when we have been hurt. An authentic apology, delivered at the correct time, heals relationships by rebuilding trust, compassion, empathy, and forgiveness. Those are lofty values, and they are available as part of every divorce and healing-from-divorce process. This is a do as I say, not as I did, lesson.

"YOU MIGHT BE RIGHT"

I admit it. I hate to admit that I'm wrong. Even when I was wrong, I have become a master of the after-the-fact justification. It is a trick of the trade, part of my cultural upbringing, and frankly one of my less desirable personality traits. I had a strong tendency to believe in the righteousness of my positions and actions. As obnoxious and arrogant as it may sound, I really thought I was "right" pretty much all the time. I rarely admitted when I was wrong. I would often justify myself or defend my position. I had a hard time even conceiving that I might be wrong. My certainty left no space for my spouse or other important people in my life to have their thoughts or feelings, which might be different from my own. This is an isolating and ineffective way to move through the world, deepen relationships, or communicate effectively.

Having a different opinion or idea doesn't mean someone is wrong. In my polarized, binary thinking, I thought that if one of us was "right" then the other must be "wrong." I was not interested in being the one who was wrong. I preferred to be right. So it was that I constructed a system of thinking and an approach to conflict with this win-lose, zero-sum-game mentality. It is no wonder that I picked an adversarial, win-lose paradigm as my professional arena. I was like the proverbial pig in muck within an adversarial divorce system. I wore that limited dualistic thinking paradigm like a badge of honor until my own divorce brought me to my knees like no previous experience in my life.

I had to learn this lesson the hard way, and I'm hoping you can learn from the error of my ways. I learned that I had a choice: I could be happy, or I could be right. Which did I prefer?

When I gave it more thought, I decided I'd rather be happy. I realized that being "right" was not all it was cracked up to be, and it made me nearly impossible to live with on a sustained basis. I learned to say the phrase, "You may be right." I remember the first time I said that to my spouse, just before we decided to divorce. I nearly gagged. It was so hard to say. I knew, strategically, I was not admitting he was right, just that he might be. This created a small opening in my certainty, which allowed me eventually to offer a full, heartfelt apology for the harm I caused him. Granted, it took me ten years post-divorce to do it, but I did it. I guess I'm a slow learner, but I felt better.

There are many ways to approach making amends. I suggest that you consider the most authentic way for you to process this concept and enlist the support of your team, whether it is your collaborative divorce lawyer, personal coach, counselor, or other collaborative divorce team members. I don't recommend doing this too soon in the process or off-the-cuff. This is a planned conversation, and you can't have an expectation of how your apology may land. This is an exercise for you.

I did not share with my spouse my list of all my wrongdoings, but I did make such a list. It was an important exercise for me to do so that I would not labor under the false impression that I was blameless in this relationship. Although it took me ten years, I eventually told my former spouse that I was truly sorry for the harm I had caused him. You may be wondering, does text count? I'd say yes, because that is what I did. I hope you can find relief sooner than that and learn from my mistakes.

There, I said it. I have made mistakes. We all do, all the time. It is natural to make a mistake. The sign of our emotional intelligence is how we choose to acknowledge those mistakes, and how quickly, so we can be relieved of the burden of shame and guilt.

Admitting I was wrong, that I had hurt my spouse (or children, or colleagues) was hard to do at first. I viewed an apology as an admission of guilt, and at a deeper level, an acknowledgment of my lack of worthiness as a human being. Being raised in a perfectionist mind-set and culture, where mistakes were something to fear and feel ashamed of, I can now see that I came to my arrogance honestly and from a place of self-protection. But as we all know, sometimes those early coping strategies no longer serve us; and at the time of a divorce, it is best to find new ways to look at yourself, your spouse, and your situation. I suggest using the lens of compassion and empathy, as opposed to self-righteousness and certainty.

With practice, I got better at this mind-set shift, and I see it as my road to freedom. I needed to learn how to release myself from my tangled web of insecurity, fear, and doubt. I needed to accept the reality that I am not perfect—that perfection is an unattainable illusion and a farce that was driving me further away from connection to others.

Once I slowed down to notice the impact my words or behaviors were having on another human being, I was appalled and embarrassed. I was mad and disappointed in myself for being so hurtful. But staying mad at myself wouldn't help and only made me feel worse. So, I set out to do the work necessary to change my attitudes and behaviors and engaged professional help. Knowing when to ask for help is a sign of emotional intelligence.

When I took time to analyze my behavior and took the focus off all of the annoying behaviors that my spouse and other people engaged in, my relationships improved. Granted, it also took me eight years after my divorce to have a friendly cup of coffee with my spouse and child, and two years more before I found myself ready and willing to offer a wholehearted apology. Better late than never as they say.

I'm sharing my experience with the hope you will find relief sooner than that and take care of this piece of emotional closure while your divorce is happening rather than a decade down the road.

I now realize that I did not come into this world to use my words as weapons, yet because of my professional training and self-protective nature, I defaulted to that behavior during my divorce. This is consistent with what I have also seen over the past thirty years of being a divorce lawyer. Using words to hurt a spouse is a common default experience. We say mean things. We write nasty e-mails in the middle of the night (tip: Do not send that e-mail to your spouse. You will regret it mightily). We justify and defend ourselves and our stories; we talk over our spouse; we don't listen well; we think we know the truth and we think we know someone else's intentions and motivations without asking if our view is even correct. This is a fascinating mind game we play. I'm suggesting that you watch out for it as you move through your divorce. Test your assumptions, especially about your spouse's actions or words.

CONFLICT HAPPENS WHEN YOU ARE NOT LISTENING

Conflict arises when people do not listen to each other. Conflict exists when we apply confirmatory biases instead of asking curious questions. Conflict exists and escalates when we apply attribution bias and shift all the blame onto someone else, instead of taking radical responsibility for our contributions to the problems. It is possible that your spouse may be stuck in a negative conflict loop with you, and you will default to your old patterns of ineffective communication. But with your new awareness (and the help of your collaborative divorce team and approach), you don't have to fall prey to it. You can make a choice not to engage in the conflict behaviors. You can openly say, "Tell me more about what you just said."

Listen to understand, not to plan your response, or justify or defend what you think you know. Try curiosity. Conflict cannot exist at the same time as curiosity. This is a concept well documented by the insight mediation movement.[3]

Bottom line: When the right time arises during your divorce process, a simple, authentic apology is a healing opportunity. It is an opportunity to accept responsibility for your contribution to the problems in your marriage that have led, at least in part, to the decision to divorce.

By now you must realize that you cannot keep blaming your spouse for everything that went wrong. Please do not let your divorce finish without making proper amends for your wrongdoing. Divorce is a time of intense personal growth and development if you choose to embrace that mind-set. There can be no growth without serious self-reflection and a healthy dose of radical self-acceptance and self-compassion for your mistakes.

But, before you can truly accept yourself, you need to accept responsibility for your contribution to the pain you caused your spouse or your children. You are not blameless. None of us can claim that status.

You can do this. This acknowledgment, even if said privately for now, opens space for an effective, authentic apology, which will ultimately lead to forgiveness and healing.

Ask your divorce professionals when might be a good time for such a conversation.

Thoughts to Consider

Have any of my choices caused harm to my spouse? Is there room to consider how my words or actions may have contributed to the fact that we are now getting divorced? Am I taking responsibility for things that are not my own or are no longer serving me? Am I willing to share this awareness with members of my team, my lawyer, or mental health professional? Am I willing to share with my spouse before the divorce process ends?

Thoughts to Let Go

I am blameless. I did nothing wrong. I don't deserve this. My spouse should suffer.

Practical Tips

Next time you sense an argument brewing, stop. Consider offering the phrase "you may be right." Stop trying to justify and defend yourself to your spouse. You are getting divorced. You don't need to do that anymore. You just need to know what you feel, what you think, and learn a way to express it so that you feel authentic, without being mean. Consult with your team members about what kind of apology or emotional closure you would like as part of your divorce. This is your divorce. Get your needs met.

8

Are You Ready to Be Divorced?

DIVORCE IS A GRIEVING PROCESS

I am more convinced than ever that divorce is a grieving process. I suggest that you start treating it like the huge loss that it is, so that you can eventually come to a peaceful acceptance of the situation and be ready, able, and willing to move on to the next stage of life. This is a positive step forward, even if it hurts, and the path is not yet clear. Accept the uncertainty and discomfort. Do not try to deny it. Denial may have worked as a self-protective mechanism in the past to shield you from painful experiences, but it only works for so long.

Let's be real: Divorce, although more common than intact marriages, feels so shameful. It feels like a failure when we live in a society where failure is not an option. Women, in particular, are burdened by perfectionism and confidence issues. Regardless of your gender, going through this process may include times when you feel like you might be dying or that your head might spin off your neck. It is very uncomfortable. I understand. You are not used to this degree of discomfort, and you may have spent many years pretending the marriage was working for you, or that this was just the way it is. The good news is that now you no longer have to pretend. The secret is out (and it can be shocking to see how your best friends saw this coming for years, yet failed to share their insights with you, and how you had no idea). It is OK. You will be fine. You will have time to process all this data.

Divorce is a decision and an experience that naturally generates fear, anxiety, anger, resentment, bitterness, and occasional bouts of hopelessness. But, as the person initiating the divorce, you have chosen to endure all of that to get out of a marriage that no longer works for you. That decision takes courage. I also understand that some of you may feel that this divorce is being thrust upon you seemingly "out of nowhere." I understand that you may be confused, angry, and perhaps feel betrayed, taken advantage of, and used. I understand your strong desire not to be made a fool in this process. No one wants to be made a fool. I would challenge you, the one who feels like a victim here, to ask yourself: how did I contribute to this? What was my role in this marriage that has now led to divorce? It is important to be honest. What do you have to lose at this point?

MANAGE YOUR LOSSES

Both of you, even the one initiating the divorce, will experience massive losses. The losses are many. You are losing your best friend, your companion and lover. You are losing the dream of your marriage. You may lose some or all of your friends (but probably not if you choose to a collaborative divorce process, as I suggest here). You may lose half of your family if your in-laws choose to take sides and disown you (again, avoidable if you choose a collaborative divorce process). One or both of you will lose your home and the comforts this represents (this is inevitable; someone must move out of the marital home, or it will be sold). You will be losing half of the time with your children whom you are used to seeing every day of their lives since birth regardless of your historic role in the family. You will lose some of your income if you were the primary wage earner. You will likely experience some loss in the standard of living unless you have sufficient wealth to avoid this financial loss.

Be clear: Just because you have money to withstand the financial loss doesn't mean you can avoid the emotional losses. Please allow yourselves time to properly grieve your losses. Perhaps the hardest loss is the fantasy that your marriage was different and that you would be together "until death do us part," just like the vow said. And as David Whyte, the poet observed, this promise will go the way "every other promise the world has made."[1] This marriage vow will now be broken, because it is time to break it.

Try not to deny the strong feelings, but also start to take control over what you can. It is important to remember that despite the divorce, you are still worthy of love. During and after a divorce, you are and can still be (in case the thought crossed your mind that you weren't) a good enough parent, a good enough lover, a good enough friend, and a good enough ex-spouse. You are not perfect. No one is. You can make a wise choice to engage in a divorce process with integrity and a positive attitude.

Social scientists and mental health professionals have written extensively on the topic of divorce and its effect on children. This book is not intended as a treatise on family law, nor is it intended to be academic or scholarly. It is my personal and professional experience and observations that I hope will help you get through your divorce with a little more grace and mutual respect than you originally thought possible. Horror stories abound. We have seen *War of the Roses*, *Marriage Story*, or *Kramer vs. Kramer* (if you haven't, you should download it for "research" purposes to see how *not* to get divorced). We have all heard from well-intentioned friends and family about how messed up their divorce was, or what a shark their divorce lawyer was and how you should use him or her for your divorce. I'm here to remind you that getting divorced with some degree of mutual respect, grace, and dignity is an achievable goal. Strive for that.

THE GRIEVING PROCESS

What is different about the collaborative divorce process from a traditional adversarial divorce process, is that as a team, we view divorce through a lens of the grieving process made popular by Elisabeth Kübler-Ross in her seminal book *On Death and Dying*.[2] The five stages of grief are denial, sadness, anger, bargaining, and acceptance.

Although never scientifically validated, for purposes of this book, divorce as a grieving process seems to fit and current scientific research supports this theory.[3] The flip side of grief is resilience and opportunity.

Why do I think that this construct applies? Divorce is a massive life transition, and it can be considered a negative psychological risk factor for children. It means that children whose parents engage in adversarial divorces and custody fights over them are at a statistically higher rate of developing problems such as anxiety, depression, suicidality, self-harm, promiscuity, drug and alcohol use/abuse. That awareness should be enough to inspire you to move through your divorce process with a higher degree of integrity and consciousness so that you protect your children from the effects of a "bad divorce."

A bad divorce is one in which you fight in court about your children. Over the course of the time it takes to get divorced, you and your spouse grow emotionally further apart, with less respect for each other and more contempt. While that is happening, your children are feeling the effects and may be stressed out. You may be so wrapped up in defending your version of reality that you may not notice. The alternative I've been suggesting is that you grow emotionally apart but in a healthy, positive way that values the other person and his or her contributions to the marriage and to your children's upbringing, and someone whom you can still call a friend, even after the divorce has been finalized.

Let's get back to the Kübler-Ross five stages of grief: denial (avoidance, confusion, elation, shock, fear), anger (frustration, irritation, anxiety), bargaining (struggling to find meaning, reaching out to others, sharing one's story and perspective), depression (feeling overwhelmed, helpless, hopeless, hostile, and wanting to run away from the pain), and acceptance (exploring options, putting together a new plan for the future, moving on).

In my experience with divorcing people, these feelings arise at some point along the continuum from when a spouse first discloses the desire for a divorce, all the way through the process, until a final order is issued by a court. How you cope with those intense emotions during your divorce is critical to emerging from this process whole, healthy, and feeling good about yourself.

GRIEF IS NOT LINEAR

The emotions come fast and furious. They come without warning, on no particular schedule, and often when you least expect them. The stages of grief are not linear. Do not expect the feelings associated with a divorce to be "neat and tidy." They are not. You may feel some but not all of these feelings. That is OK. You should know this in advance. There is no "right" way to get through this process. Do the best you can, get professional support, and be wary of anyone who tells you that it will be this way, or that way and it will last this long, or that long. No one can predict these things, and just because an "expert" says something to you, it may or may not be true, so please take all of this with a healthy grain of salt.

Here's an example: My friend once told me that for years she felt deficient because her adversarial divorce lawyer told her that "after a year" she would feel better. She took the lawyer at her word, and a year later, she was not really feeling that much better. She was still pissed-off at her husband who had cheated on her. Yes, she was divorced by then, but she was still angry. And on top of still feeling angry, she felt ashamed that she was still feeling angry, because her divorce lawyer had told her that she would be feeling better in a year. She was not fitting the mold. Here is the truth: None of us fits the mold.

Here are some common statements that suggest to me that denial is part of the divorce process: "I had no idea this was coming." "This is coming out of left field." "Wow. I did not know that my spouse was this unhappy." "I thought every marriage was sexless." "I thought we had some problems, but I didn't think they were that bad." "Come to think of it, my spouse did ask me to go to counseling about a year ago, and I think I told her she was crazy. Was that wrong?" "I thought my spouse had the problems, not me." "I cannot believe this is happening to me." "I don't think my spouse is serious about this." "I don't want to be divorced."

All that smacks of denial. It is often the case that one spouse has been thinking about a divorce for quite a long time and just never shared those thoughts. Remember, it is the breakdown in communication and accountability that often leads to divorce in the first place. So, it is also true that, at the beginning, one person "can't believe" this is happening, but the other spouse, the one initiating the divorce, is well past the denial phase. Often, that person has moved into the anger phase and is ready to put the entire marriage in the rearview mirror.

The denial phase often happens without anyone naming it, often unbeknownst to anyone in the divorce process, including the lawyers. The only person who may know this is happening is someone's therapist who, of course, cannot tell anyone. The grieving stages of divorce are not things that traditional divorce lawyers talk about with our clients, but collaborative attorneys do, which is why I am explaining it to you.

The angry phase of a divorce is everyone's worst nightmare if you are allowed to stay stuck in this mind-set and lack tools to move beyond it. This is often the time when someone "lawyers up" with the biggest shark out there, basically, to put the screws to the spouse before the other spouse does the same. This is a reactive moment. I hope this book has you thinking about new ways to respond to the news that a divorce is in your future.

The initially reactive call to the adversarial divorce lawyer is the move that leads to outrageous, expensive, and destructive adversarial divorces. If you and your spouse can just hit the pause button before reacting to your anger and fear by hiring an adversarial divorce lawyer and running to the courthouse to "file for divorce" before you have processed all of your strong emotions, I think you and your family will be better served in the long run.

My point is that your anger is a phase to work through, not get stuck in. If you don't nurture it, it may not last too long, especially if you (and/or your spouse) go to therapy. But an adversarial approach to a divorce will, no doubt, put gasoline on the fire of your anger. It will add fuel to your fear and anxiety. It may lead you to feel that you have no choice but to respond in kind, so that you don't "lose everything" to your spouse. At this point, you are sure that your spouse's aggressive lawyer is out to get you and make your life miserable—or worse, destroy you, because that is maybe what your spouse is telling you the lawyer will do to you.

People are entitled to their anger. Anger is a tough emotion, and not many of us know how to express it in an appropriate way or how to accept that another person we love is entitled to be angry at us. Many of us are natural people pleasers; we think that conflict is bad and, therefore, lack the skills to handle conflict or anger in an appropriate way.

The problem in a divorce is, if either or both of you get stuck in the angry phase and don't work through it, then anger will run the process. You will be unable to let go of your narrative. You become stuck in your emotions. It is sad to watch. Lawyers take our cues and marching orders from our clients. If you show up in a trial lawyer's office and instruct us to "protect you," to "get you the most money possible," to "get you sole custody of your children," understand that we try to satisfy what you told us were your goals. We do this, even though it may be your anger talking, not your highest and best self.

The traditional lawyer will follow the initial path you set us upon, even if your perspective changes. Perhaps you are not so angry anymore. You just want to move on in peace, because you have worked through your sadness, and you are now into acceptance. The same could be true for your spouse, especially if you have been allowed (or encouraged) to communicate freely with each other during your separation, which is more likely if you have sought the help of a separation coach. That would be great, but someone needs to tell the lawyers that you have shifted your attitude toward your spouse. I find that clients are sometimes afraid to stand up to their lawyer or assert themselves. Instead, they defer to the lawyer as the "expert" on the divorce, as opposed to the clients asserting themselves as the "experts" on their own life and marriage and how they want it to dissolve. Please assert yourselves to your lawyer if you want a peaceful divorce.

I find it fascinating that part of anger is not just frustration and irritability, but also anxiety. I have heard it said that anxiety is fear about the future, and depression is fear about the past. The bottom line, however, is that you need to deal with what is right in front of you today. The fact that your marriage is ending does not relieve you of all of your other responsibilities: to your children, your work, your community, and most important, to yourself.

Fear of the future is common at the beginning of the divorce process. You are the proverbial stranger in a strange land. You do not speak the language, and you do not know all of your options. You are processing all the losses. Our culture adds an additional layer of guilt to divorce to make it seem like divorce is someone's fault, that someone is to blame, even though we have so-called no-fault divorces. It still feels like a shameful experience that you "should" have tried harder to avoid for everyone else's benefit and comfort.

IS IT POSSIBLE THAT THIS DIVORCE IS HAPPENING FOR A GOOD REASON?

Before we get to acceptance, let's talk about bargaining, then sadness or depression. It is possible that you are relieved and happy to be getting divorced. OK. Good for you. Most people I meet in my office do not present that way.

Bargaining, as it applies to grief during a divorce, suggests that sometime during this process you will struggle to find meaning from this experience; you may want to reach out to others and share your story and perspective about it all. This is also a good time for self-reflection and a good mental health professional. It is a time to assign meaning to your life going forward, especially if you happen to be a spouse who derived not only meaning but personal identity and satisfaction from your role in the marriage. That can leave even the most sturdy among us feeling vulnerable and adrift at sea. People often tell me that they feel as if the rug has been pulled out from under them or that they have been kicked in the gut. Use any metaphor that seems appropriate. You are being asked to reconsider your entire place in the universe. That is a big deal. Sharing your perspective is helpful if you are sharing it with appropriate people. In general, your spouse is no longer your emotional go-to person, so I encourage you to find someone else who is safe and can keep your confidence.

I caution you against gossip about your ex to your friends, because it will come back to bite you. Also, it puts your friends in a difficult situation. No one knows what to do or how to handle a divorcing couple's friendships. Will you divide your friends, like you will divide the Tupperware? Will you make gatherings of your tribe uncomfortable if you are both invited? Do they have to pick sides?

The tendency is strong at some point in the divorce process for someone to try to get back together, or at least have sex. Depending on the circumstances, I will counsel accordingly. I support reconciliations. I believe in love. Sometimes those reconciliations work out. More often, they don't. That is OK. You gave it your best effort. While writing this book, I learned about a special form of couple's counseling called discernment counseling, which is specifically designed to assess the ambivalence to divorce and to connect deeply to the underlying issues that led to divorce being considered in the first place. If you are feeling ambivalent, give it a try, if you are still willing to do the work to assess whether the marriage is salvageable. That is not easy work, but none of this is easy.

Let's move on to the hardest part of the grieving process: sadness and depression. Depression is a psychiatric diagnosis. I'm not talking about clinical depression of the type that would meet the diagnostic criteria set out in the DSM-5.[4] (If you think you qualify, then you should get help. Depression is serious, and it is treatable so long as you are honest about it and do not keep it a secret. Please get help if you need it.)

For purposes of this section, I'm just talking about garden-variety sadness, even if it brings you to your knees in a puddle on the floor of your kitchen (or out in your garage or woodshop). It hurts to deal with all of this. It is stressful, and it is sad. It is also OK to feel your feelings. In fact, it is healthy to process these feelings. But it is not OK to cry all the time in front of your children. If that is happening, then please get professional help. Such chronic and intense displays of your emotions will scare your children and set them up for an unhealthy dynamic where the children will feel that it is their job to comfort you, when it needs to be the other way around.

The bottom line is that divorce is an emotionally complicated time of life. No one is immune from the huge emotional toll a divorce brings to a family. If you work through the emotional aspects of divorce, you will eventually come to acceptance.

ACCEPTANCE IS A FORM OF GRACE

True acceptance of reality is hard. It is so much easier to tell ourselves a story that we prefer to hear. But at some point in the grieving process, we wake up and say something like, "OMG, I am so sick of hearing myself talk about this." "I'm sick and tired of this story." "I'm sick and tired of feeling sick and tired." "Enough is enough. Let's get on with this divorce and move forward." When you reach that stage of your emotional roller coaster, that is a breakthrough moment worth celebrating. Once that happens, you should call your collaborative divorce lawyer and then watch the final details fall relatively neatly in place. The challenge in most divorces is that these breakthrough moments don't usually happen at the same time. So, if you have had yours, but your spouse seems stuck in some other phase of the process, your job is to focus on rebuilding your new life while being patient and demonstrating empathy for your spouse. He or she will reach where you are, on his or her time line, which cannot be rushed by arbitrary deadlines or court hearing dates.

By this time in the collaborative divorce process, when that moment of acceptance comes for both of you, the team understands that you are now ready to be divorced. You each have had the time needed to feel your feelings, obtain full and complete financial disclosures, and gain the support of your individual lawyer and the mental health coach(es), and obtain an analysis of the marital estate and retirement options from the financial neutral. Intellectually, you understand your financial reality. You understand how your emotions can be managed. You see that you and your children and your spouse will all be able to have your needs met. And you did the whole thing without going to court or threatening to go to court. You have completed a collaborative divorce and you feel satisfied that you did the absolute best you could under the circumstances. Your team bore witness to the challenges and the growth. We wish you well on this next stage of your life, and, more importantly, you can wish your spouse well too.

Thoughts to Consider

If someone I loved died, would I act this way? Would I want revenge? Would I want to make them suffer? What would happen if I try empathy? Or compassion?

Thoughts to Let Go

"I'm fine." Maybe you are, maybe you are not. Discern your truth.

Practical Tips

Deal honestly with the grief. Talk to your therapist. Do not talk about this with your spouse, as that person is no longer your emotional go-to. Often the grief is not really about the marriage or the person but is related to family-of-origin wounds or trauma. This is not easy work, but it is essential for you to move forward.

9

The Legal Logistics
What to Expect

The good news is that the number of issues involved in a divorce are finite, and this is not rocket science. The reason that divorces cost a fortune and take forever is because people are not ready to be divorced. That is why I spent this entire book trying to impress upon you the importance of dealing with the emotional aspects of your divorce first. Legally, we must address property division and income division; and, when there are minor children, parenting responsibilities and child support.

Family law is a matter of state statutes and laws. Each state will have its own peculiar ways of handling the details, which is why it is important to have sound legal advice throughout the divorce process. However, you can expect to deal with the above issues.

DIVIDING PROPERTY

When considering how to divide your property, you want to know whether you live in an "equitable division" state, or a "community property" state, or a state that recognizes "separate property." Most states have a statute that sets forth a list of elements that will be considered relevant when considering the division of property. Some of the elements include the length of the marriage; your ages and general health; your respective contributions to the marriage, both financial and nonmonetary; your ability to earn income; through whom an asset came into the marriage; and the desirability of awarding the marital home to the person who has greater responsibility for minor children.

You also want to disclose the existence of any prenuptial agreement. Prenuptial agreements are generally enforceable provided

1. disclosures were full and accurate;
2. both spouses were represented by counsel;
3. the agreement was fair when entered into; and
4. it is still equitable to enforce it at the time of the divorce.

In essence, a prenuptial agreement is a good place to start to understand your original intentions when you got married and to assess whether it is still fair and reasonable to enforce the agreement now. Sometimes it is, and sometimes it is not. Prenuptial agreements are regularly enforced, but they may not be, so it is something to consider.

Once you understand how your court approaches the division of assets in a traditional adversarial case, this knowledge will underlie the settlement process regardless of which process you choose. In a traditional divorce process, you can expect your lawyers to approach the settlement discussions or the hearings with this construct firmly in mind. They may be each arguing opposite sides of that construct and have very different ideas about how the court should interpret the facts of your case, but they will each argue that the law as applied to your facts supports the outcome that they are advocating for you. The court may or may not agree.

In a collaborative divorce process, we certainly are mindful of our state's orientation to property division. We can also be a bit more flexible, so long as the agreement is not absurd, which it will never be, because you each have a lawyer to make sure that doesn't happen.

Property division is a final settlement that cannot be modified. It has the benefit of being the one thing in a divorce settlement that cannot be renegotiated down the road. It is important that you understand the property settlement, because you will have to live with it for the rest of your life.

DIVISION OF INCOME—
ALIMONY, SPOUSAL SUPPORT, SPOUSAL MAINTENANCE

The division of income is also known as alimony, spousal support, or spousal maintenance, depending on your state. It is all the same thing, although the IRS refers to it as alimony. Alimony generally is defined as money paid from one spouse to another when the receiving spouse lacks sufficient income, property, or both to support himself or herself at a reasonable standard of living, as that standard of living was established during the marriage. The spouse being asked to pay must be able to afford it and still support himself or herself. Inability to pay is a defense to an alimony claim, but you must prove it, because no one will believe you. The systemic cynicism is borne from years of people trying to avoid paying their former spouse's alimony and engaging in a variety of shenanigans to create the appearance that they cannot afford it, when in fact, the lifestyle or standard of living belies that claim.

This is a sensitive topic. It is sensitive for the person who is being asked to pay for the support of a former spouse and it is sensitive for the person who needs the former spouse to pay support. It is the quintessential difficult conversation, and no one likes having it. But it is a part of the divorce, and it needs to be discussed and included in the conversation. Expect that it will be a part of your divorce, especially when the length of the marriage is more than five years, and where the disparity in your incomes is large.

Like property division, your state will have a statute that sets out the factors a court will consider when addressing the issue of alimony or support for a former spouse. Some of the factors include the length of the marriage (usually, the longer the marriage, the higher the entitlement); your respective incomes and the difference between the two; the need for additional training or education to be able to return to the workforce; and nonmonetary contributions to the home, including child rearing. It is well known and not controversial that women in the United States earn less than men. In fact, the Bureau of Labor Statistics's 2021 report shows that women's annual earnings were 82 percent of men's.[1]

Many states have an alimony guideline, which can help orient you to what you can expect. Alimony is generally modifiable based upon a substantial unanticipated change in circumstances. What circumstances might justify modification is something you should ask your attorney. Sometimes remarriage or cohabitation is a sufficient factor, and sometimes it is not. Sometimes not achieving the level of income that you anticipated at the time of the divorce is a sufficient change, and sometimes it is not. Because it is variable, many people like to avoid this type of future uncertainty and try to make a deal that includes more property division so that there is no alimony. This is reasonable and something to expect as part of this discussion. This is why lawyers see alimony as the flip side of the property division coin. We can negotiate a definite and larger property settlement in exchange for waiving future alimony. This is often the win-win on this issue.

PARENTING AGREEMENTS

Often the most emotionally triggering conversation is how are we going to co-parent the children. Oftentimes, one person feels like his or her entire identity is wrapped in the role of primary caregiver for children, especially in homes where the division of labor was clear. Of course, it unfair to penalize a working parent or to characterize that parent as less interested or less skillful with the children simply because he or she wasn't able to spend as much time as a parent who was able to stay home. This does not feel fair from the stay-at-home parent's perspective, because the divorce will upset the previously bargained-for division of labor. This can be a very hard pill to swallow. Often the person who stayed home to raise the children and take care of the home feels displaced and can feel a loss of identity. This is something to take very seriously in your divorce process. It is important to allow everyone to adjust to a new dynamic if maintaining the status quo is not financially feasible. Often, divorce requires that a person who previously did not work outside the home must now not only consider it, but do it. This is often not an easy transition. It takes time to come to terms with this reality. A little empathy goes a long way.

What you do not want to happen, and it can happen very easily in a divorce, is that the children become aligned with one parent or the other. This can happen in very subtle or overt ways. The parenting discussion needs to be an authentic one, in which both people need to set aside their strong feelings about the other person as a spouse and focus on what the children need. Egos should not drive this conversation, and you should expect that it may be another difficult one. Ideally, with the preparation work you have been doing in the collaborative divorce process, you have been able to experiment a bit with different parenting schedules and come to some type of equilibrium that your family can accept. No one wants to spend less time with one's children, but this is a fact of divorce.

Most states have a construct about custody that involves decision making and parenting time. It is called by different names in each state, so consult with your local attorney to understand how your state addresses issues of custody. Many states have a statute that identifies a variety of factors for a court to assess in the event of a contested custody case. These factors include each of your abilities and dispositions to provide love, affection, guidance, food, clothing, medical care and other material needs, and a safe environment; to meet the children's current and future developmental needs; the quality of the child's adjustment to current housing, school, and community, and the potential effect of any change; your ability to foster a positive relationship and promote frequent and continuing contact with the other parent, unless contact will result in abuse to the child or parent; ability to communicate effectively concerning the children; or any evidence of abuse.

Some states have presumptions of "shared" custody, and other states do not. Most parents do not want to consider themselves to be second-class citizens when it comes to parenting their children or having an unequal influence on their children's future. Whether that means a true 50/50 split is debatable, and it is up for each family to decide the best schedule of contact given the circumstances. The idea of sharing decision making is also something to discuss. Sometimes, people cannot communicate at all, and the court will have to award the decision making to one parent or the other; sometimes people have very different parenting styles. The question is whether the differences are wholly irreconcilable, or if you can each accept that the children will grow up and always be influenced by each of you and your respective families of origin. They will take some of the good stuff and some of the less desirable stuff. This is life. The research is clear: Children do best when their parents do not fight about them in a divorce. So, this is the task you are being called to resolve.

NEGOTIATIONS IN THE COLLABORATIVE PROCESS

Many books have been written about negotiation strategies. In fact, an entire industry attempts to define and strategize about how to manage conflict. A review of the literature is well beyond the scope of this book. The intensely personal nature of divorce makes it unlike any other form of dispute resolution, but some current best practices can be applied to your divorce. I am fond of Adam Kahane's approach as I distilled it from his book *Collaborating with the Enemy: How to Work with People You Don't Agree with or Like or Trust.*[2] How's that for a description of your state of mind when you are about to enter a divorce negotiation? When I first heard about this book, I thought, *how apropos* to the collaborative divorce process, which inherently supports this framework. The key takeaways for me included:

- The need for a safe, judgment-free environment to have meaningful conversations.
- No need for agreement on anything. Just show up with a willingness to listen, without planning your response.
- Embrace the polarity of conflict and connection.
- Move toward experimenting with different perspectives and possibilities and allow space for disagreement.
- Demonstrate a willingness to change; move away from trying to convince or persuade others to stop doing what they are doing or change to fit our needs, expectations, or experiences.
- Allow others the dignity of expressing their reality, their thoughts, experiences, and perceptions.

When we come to the table to discuss how we will restructure a family in one home to a family in two homes, we cannot afford to be attached to our prior ideas of how things "should be." We need to let go of our attachment to being "right" and, instead, to choose to be "happy." This is a choice. There is no single truth or right answer. In the collaborative divorce process, we are negotiating throughout the process. We help you and your spouse find new ways to create your emergent futures.

In the collaborative divorce process, you will still have the opportunity to talk about your needs and strategies with your own lawyer. The difference is that we all know that we will end up with a final agreement that will meet each of your needs. So, some strategy may be involved in terms of what to offer or what to accept. There is an expectation of further discussion regardless of the initial offers. What is fundamentally different is that the first offer will not insult your intelligence.

NEGOTIATIONS IN MEDIATION

If you do not feel the need for the supportive team approach, then you may experience negotiating with a neutral mediator. As we have discussed earlier, traditional mediations rely on interest-based negotiations, and the mediator will try to get you to "yes," whatever "yes" means for you and your spouse. It often involves some traditional negotiation strategies, which include not leading with your actual desires; keeping some information or bargaining chips close to the vest, in case you want to use them later; and generally starting higher and asking for more than you intend to get.

If you are to find a mediator who has been trained in a more collaborative approach to negotiation and mediation, called insight mediation, then you will experience a different type of mediation. The mediator will be conscious of the fact that curiosity and conflict cannot exist in the same moment. The mediator will be looking for ways that you seem to be emotionally triggered and will gently (or not so gently) probe to understand what the underlying concern is, so that you can express it honestly and then the issue can be put on the table for acknowledgment. If you are a collaborative professional, and you are looking for resources to consider for additional training, I recommend checking out our friend from Prince Edward Island, Jacinta Gallant, who is taking innovation for collaborative lawyers to the next level.[3]

FINALIZING THE DEAL

Once the terms of the final settlement are reached, they are reduced to a written, legally binding document that you and your spouse sign. The paperwork will be prepared and then submitted to the court for an uncontested divorce.

Then the choice is yours as to how to say good-bye to each other, the marriage, and the collaborative team.

Thoughts to Consider

How much support do I need in this process, emotional, legal, and financial? Do I feel like I am on equal bargaining footing with my spouse? If not, what could help me understand better and feel more confident when we get to final negotiations? I can handle this.

Thoughts to Let Go

I will never get this. I don't understand what is happening. I'm afraid I will be taken advantage of, or I am afraid to ask for the help I need.

Practical Tips

Talk to your lawyer about any concerns during your divorce process. Your lawyer is your guide and is there to help.

Part III

YOUR EMERGENT FUTURE IS NOW

10

Move Confidently Forward into Your Future

> The power of attention is the real superpower of our age. Attention, aligned with intention, can make mountains move. —Otto Scharmer[1]

I understand that it is hard to think about your future when you are just starting a divorce process. I'm asking you to lift your eyes up over the horizon. What can you see? Take time to visualize yourself. Do you see yourself feeling healthy and fit, surrounded by love, by friends and family who care about your well-being and with whom you can be your authentic self in all your glory and your goofiness, your sweetness and your sorrows, your fierceness and your vulnerabilities? I want you to feel connected with the rest of humanity. Somehow, I've noticed, the traditional divorce process tends to isolate us and put us in binary roles of victim or perpetrator. We may even become martyrs of self-sacrifice, as if our needs are not as important as everyone else's.

Start to think about yourself and what you need to make that vision for yourself a reality. I'm suggesting that your future is entirely dependent on how you handle yourself right now, from this moment forward. You can change your attitude and reframe anything that is happening. It starts with noticing where you put your attention. As Otto Scharmer observed, "There is no such thing as the future. We all know that the future is not what happens to us . . . the future is what we do with what happens to us." In other words, your emergent future is now.[2] Are you thinking, *what on earth is this woman talking about?*

As some of you may know or guess about me, although a lawyer by calling, training, and profession, I've been a philosopher at heart my entire life. Since my divorce, I've been trying to make meaning of my life. How did I end up surrounded by divorce in both my personal and professional life? What I noticed early in my divorce process was that how my post-divorce life would unfold would be entirely my responsibility. No longer could I conveniently defer to my former spouse's worldview, choices, or decisions, then silently resent that I was not doing what I truly wanted or justify my negative attitude because of what he was doing or how he was feeling. Learning about co-dependency, boundaries, and self-care were essential building blocks to restore my self-esteem, which I hadn't noticed was lacking.

If I was uncomfortable with how I was behaving, then it was my responsibility to change. If I was unsatisfied in my professional adversarial litigation practice, then it was my responsibility to change. I realized that for the first time in my adult life, I was on my own. This can be both exhilarating and terrifying. This is when I started to explore the world of professional coaches or teachers . . . a personal trainer, a business coach, a spiritual coach . . . are you getting my drift? Just because change is my responsibility doesn't mean that I had to do it alone. In fact, doing anything alone is virtually impossible. It takes the help of other people who love what they do to help you find what it is you love to do. Whether you want to have a good divorce or change another significant aspect of your life, help is available if you ask for it. Now is not the time to be shy.

Once I realized the awesome responsibility and opportunity this change presented, I wanted to meet it in the best way possible for me and my daughter. I felt an enormous responsibility to ensure that my daughter would come through our divorce not only intact, but I wanted her to thrive despite the divorce. I knew she was watching me, and that I would be her primary influence. This motivated me, big time.

In what seemed at the time a random invitation, but which I now see as the catalyst for this book, I was exposed to new disciplines that I had never heard of, such as organizational development, transformational organizational development, systems theory, executive leadership, and the ways in which leadership principles and theories of adult development could help me grow as a person and leader. I realized that my personal growth would, in turn, help my clients work through the complexity of their divorce. I became a student of how organizations, systems, and the people within them change or don't, depending on the willingness of the leaders within the system to set aside their egos and start to listen more deeply. I started to understand that a good leader must question what he thinks is true and how it could be wrong. I realized that leaders must be willing to overcome their own resistance to change.³ I realized that we are all leaders of our own lives, whether we are running large businesses, small businesses, classrooms, or homes.

My exceptional colleague and friend Susan Palmer⁴ invited me into mighty conversations taking place across the globe. At first, my curiosity was piqued because I was fascinated to learn why people say they want to change but often don't. I found that these leadership concepts could have a practical application, not just at the organization level, of which I had very little experience, but at the individual level, starting with me. I stayed in these conversations, and I listened.

DIVORCE IS A TRANSFORMATIONAL GROWTH OPPORTUNITY

There is no doubt: You have a choice about how your divorce will uplift and empower you and your children, if you have them, or ruin you with ruminations about how your spouse screwed up your life and how you may never forgive him or her. These are all choices of the mind—your mind. And they are choices of the heart—your heart.

My therapist gave me some sound advice at the time of my divorce, which I have shared with my clients over the years. He told me that I have control over very few things in my life, except what I put in my mouth, what comes out of my mouth, where my feet take me, and what I think about. Well, that broke it down clearly for me.

I encourage you to transform your current pain into the catalyst for the next stage of your brilliant life. You have a gift to share. We all do. Some of us simply have not been encouraged to explore it, so I want to give you that permission. What does that even look like, you might ask? It is different for everyone, but what have you been curious about lately? Where do you feel safe and most authentically yourself? When was the last time you felt joy?

When the leadership conversations turned to joy, I was truly stumped. I had not experienced joy in so many years, I had forgotten what that even felt like. So, I set an intention and began an earnest exploration of the concept of joy and how to embody it. I'm the type of learner who first needs to understand something cognitively before I can let myself relax enough to feel it as a sensation. I found *The Book of Joy* to be a helpful resource, as the Dalai Lama and Desmond Tutu struck me as reliable sources.[5] Spoiler alert: Joy is not just an emotion; it's a state of being that they describe as four pillars of the mind (perspective, humility, humor, acceptance) and four pillars of the heart (forgiveness, gratitude, compassion, generosity).

Can you see how applying the eight pillars to your collaborative divorce process will likely result in an outcome that is completely different from engaging in an adversarial war with your spouse? Can you imagine having a moment of levity with your spouse during your team meeting? Can you see how gaining a realistic perspective on your needs and those of your spouse more likely will enable them to be met? Do you see how humility, not humiliation, could be a useful character trait as you explore the unknown territory of a divorce process with the help of a team of divorce sherpas who know how to carry you up this mountain? I hope you can see how acceptance is the key to serenity, and how you cannot begin the final step of making the final settlement agreements until you have both accepted the truth—that this divorce is the right thing for you both and for your family. You can co-create your divorce process with your collaborative team members so that you can once again flex the muscles of your heart to allow your compassion, forgiveness, gratitude, and generosity to emerge.

From my perspective, this is what a collaborative case is all about. Why we are not all doing this, I really do not understand, although I do have theories about it, of course. The wise among you will see how you can apply the eight pillars of joy to your divorce and to your life now. By doing so, you have a greater chance of emerging from this divorce better than you entered. How could you not?

SELF-CARE

What have you done for your self-care lately? A bath, a walk in the woods, a quiet couple of hours on the couch reading a book? A game? A connection with a friend or animal? A coloring book, a new paint set, a meditation practice to become aware of your racing thoughts? A nap? It is time to take care of yourself, whatever that means for you.

LOOK HOW FAR YOU HAVE COME

When you get to the end of your divorce process, take a moment and reflect on where you were when you started and where you are now. There will be a change. Change is inevitable. It is the only constant in life that you can rely on. Things are always in a state of flux and change. Remember old Heraclitus, who is attributed with saying that no one steps in the same river twice? Each moment of each day is an opportunity to start fresh. Even if you lost it, on your children or your former spouse, you could make an amends and start over. It is OK. As you now can see, divorce is a process and a state of mind. Consider that this is all happening to teach you some bigger lesson for your benefit. When in doubt, perhaps this Rumi poem will help:

The Guest House

This being human is a guest house.
Every morning a new arrival.

A joy, a depression, a meanness,
Some momentary awareness comes
as an unexpected visitor.

Welcome and entertain them all!
Even if they're a crowd of sorrows,
who violently sweep your house
empty of its furniture,
still, treat each guest honorably.
He may be clearing you out
for some new delight.

The dark thought, the shame, the malice,
meet them at the door laughing
and invite them in.[6]

THE POSSIBILITIES FOR YOUR FUTURE AS CO-PARENTS AND FRIENDS EVEN IN THE FACE OF INFIDELITY

If you choose a collaborative divorce process, or at least the principles, you will have the opportunity to create new rituals, especially if you want to stay connected. You can spend time thinking about how the holidays will look, if not forever, at least for this year. You may need the coach's help to have an honest, authentic discussion about what this could look like. The possibilities are as endless as your imaginations.

If you are struggling with the impact of an extramarital affair, or whether to share that information as part of your collaborative process, I encourage you to read Esther Perel's book *The State of Affairs: Rethinking Infidelity* for a perspective that may help you process the feelings of betrayal and guilt. Interestingly, she notes, "Once divorce carried all the stigma. Now, choosing to stay when you could leave is the new shame."[7] So, just because there has been an infidelity doesn't mean you must get divorced.

I'm tired of all the shame and blame of traditional knee-jerk reactions. Even when a marriage has been affected by infidelity, the collaborative model can help you talk about it. It is likely to stir up a lot of feelings, which if left unattended can lead to a lot of destruction and hurt feelings. If you are hiding an extramarital affair, however you wish to define it, it is probably a good idea to talk about it with your attorney. Your collaborative attorney is the only one on the team who can assure you of confidentiality. So, if you need to share with someone, your lawyer or your personal therapist is the place to go, so you can get wise counsel about how this may impact your divorce.

In my experience, it is not required to disclose an affair during the collaborative process, unless the failure to disclose will directly impact the case from moving forward. Sometimes something happened in the past that has no impact on the current conversation, and perhaps it is not necessary to disclose it after the fact. That is a different situation than someone who is currently engaged in a new relationship, which will soon be disclosed, and may have an impact on the children, for example; or if your spouse is soon likely to hear about this from a family member or the internet. In that case, your collaborative attorney will likely strongly encourage you to disclose so that the issue is on the table for processing and discussion.

The conversation about new relationships or sexual attractions during the divorce are hard but necessary for you and your spouse. Issues will arise about how, when, or whether to introduce a new person into the newly rearranging family structure. Much will depend on the individual circumstances, so I won't spend much more time on this issue. This is a delicate conversation that needs the guidance of skillful professionals.

One last thought from an attorney who has been on both sides of this issue many times throughout my career: First, the adversarial system in most jurisdictions does not care about an affair in terms of impact on the financial or division of parenting time. Second, in the collaborative model, regardless of which spouse I represent, I always prefer to have a colleague talk to the other spouse about ways to work through the news of the affair and how to separate the emotional reactions from the day-to-day requirements of communication or co-parenting. If I represent the person who is just receiving the news, I can offer support and perspective to help the client move through and beyond it. If I represent the person having an extramartial affair, I encourage disclosure sooner rather than later. I always prefer to have these conversations in the safety of a collaborative team, for both clients' sake. No matter which side of the issue, my client will be protected by the collaborative team from the typical shaming that would occur in a traditional divorce. This seems to me to be a healthy and mature way to move forward.

DATING AND YOUR NEXT RELATIONSHIP

Depending on whether you initiated the divorce, or were the one in an extramarital affair, or the one who still can't believe this is happening to you, at some point in the not-too-distant future, you will start dating again. It is just a fact of life and, frankly, it should be celebrated. I am not a dating expert. I'm just a divorce lawyer. What I can say, professionally, is that you do not want to introduce your children to anyone you are dating when you are still going through the legal and emotional logistics of getting your divorce settled. Discretion is the name of the dating game during divorce. You don't want to add fuel to the fire. It also relates to how this person you are dating fits into your next stage of life. Are you dating for fun, with no expectation of a long-term relationship? This is a different situation than someone who is starting a new "relationship"; it is different still if the "new" relationship is a person you have been dating during your marriage, or during your divorce process, as opposed to waiting until your divorce is over.

If you are both comfortable talking about sexuality and dating during the divorce, then start talking. Anything you can do to make this inevitable situation easier for both of you will help. If you are not so skillful in talking about sex, then it is in your best interests to talk with someone who can help you sort out your new sexual self, now that you are free. You have important questions to consider: Do I want to know if my spouse is dating? Do I want to know who my spouse is dating? Am I entitled to know these things, or is it none of my business? Do we have an agreement about introducing new partners to the children? Do you get to meet the new partner before the children do, so that you don't hear about this new person from them? Does it make sense to have an arbitrary time line before introducing the children, or can you be more flexible and trust your former spouse enough to choose to be with someone who is good for your spouse and will be kind and supportive of you and your children? Will this new person pose a threat to your security, even after you are divorced, or can this person be integrated into your family, especially if he or she will be helping your spouse with parenting issues as time goes on? How do you manage the conversation to make sure that the new partner doesn't try to usurp your role? How do you manage feelings of jealousy? All of these are important questions to consider and talk about in your divorce process when you are ready to do so.

If you do not talk about dating, new relationships and roles of the new partners, then when it happens, it once again will feel like a shock, and you could set back your emotional progress.

PRENUPTIAL AGREEMENTS IF YOU DECIDE TO REMARRY

First, I want to applaud your romantic optimism to consider getting married for a second time. Statistically, you are at a higher risk for divorce the more times you try marriage. So, if you are thinking about getting married again, remember how challenging your first divorce was, how hard you had to work to get the settlement that you received. Protect it with a prenuptial agreement. I know it doesn't sound very romantic to have a conversation about how to divide money in the event of a divorce before you get married, but it can be a helpful communication exercise with your new spouse. If you have children, minor or adult from a prior relationship, your children will thank you down the road if you end up divorced.

A prenuptial agreement is very common. It is a legally binding document that sets out what should happen in case this new marriage ends up in a divorce. A prenuptial agreement is not 100 percent guaranteed to be enforced. But your chances of it being followed increase as long as you address the following:

- You each have your own independent attorney represent you in the prenuptial agreement negotiation so that it is free and voluntary, and there is no duress;
- There is a full and complete financial disclosure of all assets, liabilities, and incomes;
- The agreement is fair and reasonable when entered; and
- The agreement is fair and reasonable when enforcement is sought.

The standard for reasonableness is not overly burdensome. Basically, your agreement cannot leave one spouse as a ward of the state. Ideally, you can see how you and your spouse will take care of each other, in the event of a divorce. It can be an opportunity to assess each other's generosity.

Often, people wish to keep separate various assets and not co-mingle them with a new spouse. Does this include the appreciation in value of these assets? What if you are moving into a house that one spouse owned but the other makes contributions, financial or nonmonetary? Will there be a provision for sharing in the appreciation of equity? What if one of you is ready to retire and one of you gives up a career? Will there be compensation, alimony or otherwise, depending on how long the marriage lasts? It is important to talk about your anticipated future financial reality when you are entering a second marriage, and it is important to consult an attorney in your state.

Using a collaboratively trained divorce lawyer is a good place to start when you need to draft a prenuptial agreement. The lawyer's training and experience with divorce are ideal for helping you and your future betrothed to have what can be a difficult conversation about money and lifestyles before you get married. This can be an awkward conversation, but often the folks who discuss money before they get married, who have a prenuptial agreement, won't need it. But, if you do need it, you want the prenuptial agreement to be the baseline, and you want it to be enforceable. If you end up divorcing, you can always choose to be more generous than the prenuptial agreement, but as least you will know what to expect if you have a solidly drafted agreement.

CONCLUSION

Competent legal counsel has no substitute. Although nothing I have shared with you is intended as legal advice, and no attorney-client relationship has been created, I feel grateful for the opportunity to share my perspective on divorce. These thoughts are my own, and I am totally responsible for the content. If you wish to reach out, I'm happy to consult with you and to help you find the resources you need to have a healthy, amicable, non-adversarial divorce. You deserve it. So does your family. Everyone will thank you for doing the hard work of divorcing with dignity.

Thoughts to Consider

This is now your life. How you behave is up to you. You are creating your future by your actions today.

Thoughts to Let Go

"If only" thoughts (i.e., if only I were younger, prettier, smarter, sexier, funnier, etc.). Time to let all of that go. Embrace yourself and who you are becoming, independent from your prior identity as a spouse.

Practical Tips

Surround yourself with people, places, and activities that bring you joy. You deserve it.

Appendix A

Road Map of the Collaborative Divorce Process*

Both of you want to be treated fairly. "Fair" is a very subjective idea. However, careful preparation and good communication can facilitate and perhaps shorten the process and help us achieve an outcome that is satisfactory to both parties. We have developed the road map to help you understand the process and show where you are at any given time.

The precise course of your particular case will vary depending upon several factors, including your individual needs, the complexity of the finances, whether you have children and, if so, their needs.

WARNINGS

- Failure to do your assignments in a timely way will cost additional time and money.
- Deviating from the road map may cost additional time and money.
- Failure to use your coach to assist you in managing your emotions will cost additional time and money.

STAGE ONE: SIGNING ON TO THE PROCESS AND ASSEMBLING THE TEAM

1.1 Clients meet and hire attorneys.
1.2 Attorneys confer regarding assembling the team.
1.3 Clients select coaches.

*Reprinted with permission of Collaborative Practice Vermont (CPVT).

1.4 First four-way meeting at which:

> participation agreement and release signed.
> road map reviewed.
> valuation date discussion.
> cost of collaborative divorce and discussion of how it will be paid.
> schedule first financial meeting.
> schedule financial five-way and other appropriate meetings.
> set up any temporary children/cash flow arrangements.

1.5 Clients meet coaches and hire them.

1.6 Clients meet with financial specialist and begin financial information assembly.

1.7 Professionals conference call to assess case and develop overall timing of the case.

STAGE TWO: COMMUNICATE AND GATHER INFORMATION REGARDING CHILDREN AND FINANCES

A better outcome is reached after you completely understand your financial situation and the best way to help your children. This stage involves the exchange of all necessary information and creates a good foundation for decision making.

Children and Communications

2.1 Coaches meet with you individually and determine whether to use a child specialist or have the coaches handle this work. Child specialist selected, if indicated, and meets with parents.

2.2 Coaches have regular check-in with you and meet with you as needed to stay centered and develop a sense of priorities.

2.3 Coaches four ways, as indicated, to develop parenting plan and facilitate communication. These will be ongoing sessions throughout the process.

2.4 Child specialist meets with your children (if applicable).

Finances

2a.1 You jointly provide all necessary financial information.

2a.2 You jointly meet with financial specialist to understand data.

2a.3 Financial meeting for presentation of financial picture and determination of what additional appraisal or assessment work is necessary.

2a.4 Additional appraisals or assessment work undertaken and completed: assemble all financial information for a complete financial picture.

2a.5 Additional financial meetings, if needed.

2a.6 Professional conference call to decide who should be present at which meetings during Stage 3 and discuss any issues that have developed.

STAGE THREE: IDENTIFYING INTERESTS AND CONCERNS

Both of you want an outcome that meets your most important concerns; in this stage, we take explore your values, concerns, and priorities so that we will be better able to find a mutually acceptable resolution. Instead of getting locked into positions, we need to develop possibilities to help us find common ground to reach resolution.

3.1 Preparation: You will meet with your attorney and possibly coach to identify your interests and priorities.

3.2 Interest meeting: You will meet as appropriate to discuss and understand each other's individual interests and priorities; group brainstorming regarding possible solutions.

3.3 You meet separately and/or together with appropriate professional team members to review the possible solutions that were developed during brainstorming to develop options for consideration and review implications of different possibilities.

3.4 You meet jointly in a five-way meeting with the child specialist and your coaches for feedback from the child specialist (if applicable).

3.5 Professionals conference call to discuss financial and parenting decision-making process, including who should be present and responsible for leading each effort.

STAGE FOUR: MAKING DECISIONS

Having done all our homework well, we are now ready to reach conclusions that meet the needs of both of you (and your children). To do this, we need to have an orderly exchange of ideas and proposals and continue the conversation until we find a result that both of you can accept.

4.1 You meet jointly with attorneys and other professionals as appropriate and necessary to present several financial packages, identifying the interests served for each person by each of the possible solutions.

4.2 You have settlement meetings as needed with professionals to come to a conclusion regarding the financial plan—these are solutions that are good for you, your spouse, and your family.

4.3 You meet with your coaches (or as otherwise arranged) to develop final parenting plan.

4.4 Professional conference call: Inform all team members of outcome and identify recommendations for couple for future. Team debriefing.

STAGE FIVE: FINALIZING AND IMPLEMENTING THE PLAN

To complete the process, decisions may need to be made about timing and the implementation of the agreement. In order to complete our work, appropriate documents need to be signed by both parties.

5.1 You jointly agree which attorney will draw up the agreement and whether to divorce immediately or wait; paperwork is drawn up by attorneys.

5.2 You jointly meet with the attorneys to revise and sign property settlement/separation agreement and any ancillary paperwork (deeds, titles, etc.) and discuss any recommendations from the team. All professionals should be paid in full before the signing occurs.

5.3 File divorce paperwork and upon receipt of final order, draft and file a QDRO (qualified domestic relations order) if necessary. Case is closed.

Appendix B

(Sample) Collaborative Divorce Participation Agreement*

GOALS

We, _____ and _____, the participants, believe that it is in our best interests to resolve differences and reach agreement through the collaborative divorce process instead of going to court. In using the collaborative divorce process, we rely on an atmosphere of honesty, cooperation, integrity, professionalism, dignity, respect, and candor to satisfy our interests and to find acceptable solutions.

GOOD-FAITH NEGOTIATION

We agree to take a balanced approach to resolving all differences and will use our best efforts to work together to create acceptable solutions. Although we may discuss the likely outcome of going to court, we will not use threats of litigation as a way of forcing settlement. We will respect each other and work to protect the privacy and dignity of everyone involved in the collaborative divorce process. We will maintain the highest standard of integrity and will not take advantage of any miscalculations or mistakes of others but will identify and correct them immediately.

WE WILL NOT GO TO COURT

1. *Out of Court.* We commit to resolving all issues without going to court.

*Reprinted with permission of Collaborative Practice Vermont (CPVT).

2. **Disclosure.** We agree to act in good faith to give full, accurate, and complete disclosure of all information whether requested or not. We will make requests for information informally and provide all information promptly. We may request this information be disclosed in affidavit form. We acknowledge that by using the collaborative process, we are giving up certain discovery procedures and methods available to us in the litigation process. We give up these measures with the specific understanding that we will make full and fair disclosure of all income, assets, debts, and other information necessary for a fair settlement.

3. **Settlement Conferences.** We agree to engage in informal discussions and conferences to settle all issues. We will focus on parenting, financial and property issues, and the constructive resolution of these issues. We understand and acknowledge the substantial cost of settlement meetings and agree to make the best use of time constraints and financial resources and to avoid unnecessary discussions of past events. We will not make accusations or claims not based in fact.

4. **Other Discussions.** We may discuss issues outside of the settlement meetings if we agree and are comfortable doing so. We may also insist these discussions be reserved for settlement meetings when both lawyers or a neutral is present. We agree not to "spring" discussions on the other in unannounced telephone calls or surprise visits to the other's residence.

CAUTIONS

1. **Commitment.** There is no guarantee that we will resolve our differences successfully with the collaborative divorce process. Success is dependent primarily on our commitment to the process.

2. **Legal Issues.** The collaborative divorce process is designed to resolve legal issues such as health and life insurance, spousal support, division of property and debt, parenting agreements, lawyer's fees and costs, and any other issues we may agree to discuss.

3. **Other Issues.** This process is not designed to address therapeutic or psychological issues. When these or other nonlegal issues arise, our lawyers or mental health professional (coach) may refer us to appropriate experts or consultants.

4. *Participants' Roles.* We pledge to be respectful and negotiate a fair resolution of all issues. However, we are each entitled to assert our respective interests, and our lawyers will help us do this in a productive manner.

5. *Lawyer's Roles.* Each lawyer has a professional duty to represent her or his own client diligently and is not the lawyer for the other, even though each lawyer shares a commitment to the collaborative divorce process. If the collaborative divorce process terminates, neither lawyer can represent either party in future litigation.

6. *Role of Mental Health Professional.* The mental health professional (coach) will participate in meetings to help us prioritize present and future concerns and goals. The coach will assist us in managing our stress level and emotions during the collaborative process so that we continually move toward an agreement in a productive manner. The coach will not serve as a therapist for either of us, or our family. If either of us needs extra support, the coach will recommend services outside of the collaborative process.

PROFESSIONAL FEES AND COSTS

We agree that our lawyers will be paid for their services and that each of us will pay our own lawyer unless otherwise agreed during the collaborative divorce process that one of us will contribute to the other's lawyer's fees or marital assets will be used to pay the fees.

We agree that our mental health professional (coach) and financial neutral, if any, will be paid for his or her services and that the neutrals will be retained and paid for jointly unless we agree otherwise in writing.

EXPERTS

1. We agree to use mental health professionals, neutral experts, or other consultants as appropriate and necessary. We will retain experts jointly unless we agree otherwise in writing. We will agree in advance as to the source of payment for the expert's retainer and other fees. We agree to direct all experts to cooperate in resolving all issues without litigation.

2. Unless otherwise agreed in writing, the neutral expert or consultant and any report or other documents or recommendations generated by, or any oral communication from, the expert will be shared with each of us and covered by the confidentiality clause of this agreement.

RIGHTS AND OBLIGATIONS PENDING SETTLEMENT

Although we agree to work outside the judicial system, we agree to be bound by the following provisions ordinarily issued as orders by the family court, unless we agree otherwise in writing, while the collaborative divorce process is pending.

1. *Marital Property*. We agree not to sell, transfer, conceal, damage, mortgage, or dispose of any asset. Assets include all real and personal property in which either of us has an interest, such as motor vehicles, bank accounts, stock and other securities, retirement accounts and pension plans.
2. *Insurance Policies*. We agree to maintain all insurance policies in effect. Insurance includes medical, dental, life, disability, automobile, homeowners, and rental insurance.
3. *Utilities*. We agree to maintain all utility services in effect. Utility services include telephone, internet, gas, electric, oil, cable and satellite TV.

ABUSE OF THE COLLABORATIVE DIVORCE PROCESS

We understand that the collaborative divorce process must terminate if either lawyer learns that either of us has taken unfair advantage of this process. Some examples are:

1. Refusing to comply with any provision of the Rights and Obligations Pending Settlement section.
2. Withholding or misrepresenting relevant information. Refusing to disclose the existence or true nature of income, assets, or debts.

3. Taking any action to undermine or take unfair advantage of the collaborative divorce process.

ENFORCEABILITY OF AGREEMENTS

1. ***Temporary Agreements***. If either of us requires a temporary agreement for any purpose, we will put the agreement in a writing signed by us and our lawyers.
2. ***Final Agreements***. If we sign a final agreement, we shall submit the final agreement to the court as the basis for entry of a final order.
3. ***In Case of Termination***. If the collaborative divorce process is terminated for any reason, we may file any written temporary agreement with the court as the basis for an order retroactive to the date of the written agreement. Similarly, we may file any final agreement with the court as the basis for a final order.

LEGAL PROCESS

1. ***No Court***. We will not initiate a court action during the collaborative divorce process unless otherwise agreed in writing in advance of such action.
2. ***Final Stipulation***. After we reach a final agreement, our lawyers will prepare a final stipulation for review and signing by us and our lawyers, unless otherwise agreed in writing.
3. ***Successful Conclusion of Collaborative Divorce Process***. We will file the appropriate action and a fully executed final agreement, and other necessary documents upon the successful conclusion of the collaborative divorce process, unless otherwise agreed in writing.

WITHDRAWAL FROM COLLABORATIVE DIVORCE PROCESS

1. ***Participant Withdrawal***. If one of us decides to withdraw from the process, s/he shall provide prompt written notice to her/his

lawyer, who in turn will provide prompt written notice to the other lawyer. Withdrawal of one of us will terminate the collaborative divorce process.

2. ***Withdrawal of Professional.***

   A. If one of our lawyers decides to withdraw from the process, s/he will provide prompt written notice to her/his client and to the other lawyer. Notice of withdrawal automatically terminates this process unless the participant whose lawyer has withdrawn notifies the other participant and her/his lawyer of her/his intention to continue the collaborative divorce process; and within 30 days of the notice of withdrawal, retains a new lawyer who will agree to be bound by this agreement or informs the other participant and her/his lawyer s/he intends to proceed without a lawyer.

   B. If the mental health professional (coach) or other neutral professional decides to withdraw from the process, s/he will provide prompt written notice to the lawyers. Notice of withdrawal of a neutral professional does not automatically terminate this process unless the neutral professional informs the lawyers that there has been an abuse of the process as defined above and either one or both lawyers believes that termination is required under the terms of this agreement.

3. ***Return of Files.*** Upon termination of the process, the lawyers will return the files to their respective clients, excluding lawyer work product.

4. ***Waiting Period.*** Upon termination of the process, we agree to wait 30 days (unless there is an emergency) to initiate court action or appear at a hearing, to permit each of us to retain new lawyers and to make an orderly transition.

5. ***Previous Agreements.*** All temporary agreements will remain in full force and effect during any waiting period.

6. ***Presentation to the Court.*** We agree that in requesting a postponement of a hearing scheduled by the other party during the 30-day waiting period, either of us may bring this provision of the collaborative divorce agreement to the attention of the court.

CONFIDENTIALITY

All settlement proposals exchanged within the collaborative divorce process will be confidential and without prejudice. If subsequent litigation occurs, we agree:

1. We will not introduce as evidence information disclosed during the process for purposes of reaching settlement, except documents and information otherwise permitted or compelled by law, including sworn statements as to financial status.

2. We will not introduce as evidence information disclosed during the process with respect to the other's behavior or legal position during the process.

3. We will not depose either lawyer, mental health professional, or any neutral expert, or ask or subpoena either lawyer, mental health professional, or any neutral expert to testify in any court proceeding as to matters disclosed during the collaborative divorce process.

4. We will not require any notes, records, or documents in the possession of either lawyer, mental health professional, or any neutral expert to be produced at any court proceeding.

PEER REVIEW WAIVER

As part of professional development and quality assurance, members of (INSERT PRACTICE GROUP) including lawyers, mental health professionals, and financial planners participate in peer review and consultation. We agree that the professional members of our collaborative team may consult with the members of the practice group regarding our collaborative proceeding. If they do so, they will make all efforts to retain our anonymity.

ACKNOWLEDGMENT

We, our lawyers, and other professional team members have read this agreement, understand its terms and conditions, and agree to abide by them.

1. We understand that by agreeing to this alternative method of resolving our family issues, we are giving up certain rights, including formal discovery, court hearings, and other procedures provided by the adversarial legal system.
2. We have chosen the collaborative divorce process to reduce emotional and financial costs and to prepare a final agreement that addresses our concerns. We will work in good faith to achieve this goal.

Client   Date   Client   Date

TEAM PROFESSIONALS

We acknowledge and undertake to use our skills and our professional training to assist the parties to give full force and effect to the terms of this agreement, and we agree to be bound to the terms herein as professional team members.

_____   _____
, Esq.   Date

_____   _____
, Esq.   Date

_____   _____
Professional   Date

_____   _____
Professional   Date

Appendix C

Why Have a Mental Health Coach?*

Help us present our "best selves" in the collaborative process.

Assist us to identify and prioritize concerns and goals for ourselves and our family now and in the future.

Work to reduce our level of stress and manage our emotions related to the divorce.

Help us develop effective communication and when there are children, co-parenting skills.

Support us in dealing with different levels of acceptance/feelings and attitudes about the divorce.

Assist us to develop a shared narrative for extended family, friends, and the children, if any.

Work collaboratively with each of us, our attorneys, and other involved professionals to anticipate problems and resolve problems as they arise.

Help our attorneys understand our individual emotional "hot spots," fears, and concerns.

Help our attorneys understand the impact of the marital dynamic on the collaborative process in creating impasse, stalling, and positional behaviors.

Help our attorneys and other team members resist being drawn into our dynamic as a couple or positions.

Make real-time interventions during meetings to identify psychological roadblocks.

Facilitate focused and efficient pacing of meetings and process.

Assist us to stay focused on the present and the future.

*Reprinted with permission of Collaborative Practice Vermont (CPVT).

Normalize our intense emotions so we can remain active and able to
think creatively and without taking a position.

Assist us in generating and evaluating options in parenting and sometimes financial meetings.

Guide and enforce the structure of the collaborative process with us
and assist the professional team in promoting the collaborative
process.

Help us make the transition from an emotionally engaged couple to
a business/problem-solving relationship and help us co-parent if
applicable.

We further understand that the mental health professional/coach is
not providing individual or couple's therapy and will not serve as a
therapist for either of us, or any member of our family before, during, or
after the process. When children are involved, we understand the mental
health professional will work with both of us (or with the assistance of
a child specialist) to develop child-focused parenting plans that take
into consideration professional expertise in child development and the
psychological impact of divorce on family members. We agree to the
above purposes and have separately executed a retainer agreement with
our agreed-upon mental health professional/coach, and agree to the
terms contained therein.

_____   _____

Client   Date

_____   _____

Client   Date

Appendix D

Collaborative Practice: How It Works for the Client*

Collaborative Practice – How it Works for the Client
With thanks to Collaborative Divorce Team Trainings

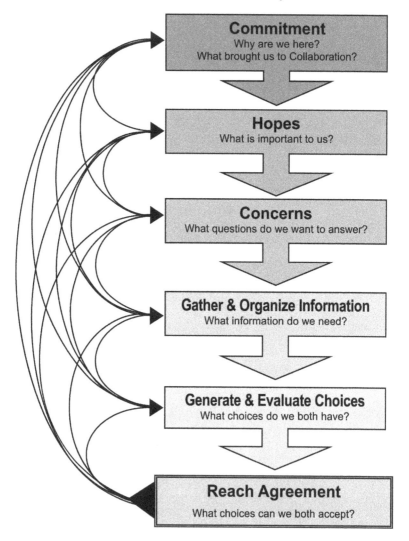

*Reprinted with permission of Collaborative Practice San Mateo County (CPSMC).

Appendix E

Collaborative Process*

Appendix E

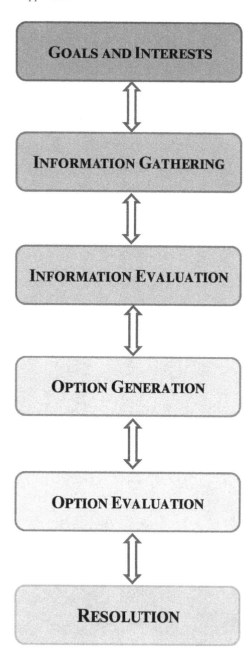

*Reprinted with permission of Collaborative Practice San Mateo County (CPSMC).

Notes

INTRODUCTION

1. Stuart G. Webb and Ron Ousky, *The Collaborative Way to Divorce: The Revolutionary Method That Results in Less Stress, Lower Costs, and Happier Kids—Without Going to Court* (New York: Hudson Street Press, 2006).

2. Pauline H. Tesler and Peggy Thompson, *Collaborative Divorce: The Revolutionary New Way to Restructure Your Family, Resolve Legal Issues, and Move on with Your Life* (New York: William Morrow, 2007).

3. Kate Scharff and Lisa Herrick, *Navigating Emotional Currents in Collaborative Divorce: A Guide to Enlightened Team Practice* (Chicago: American Bar Association, 2011).

4. International Academy of Collaborative Professionals, www.collaborativepractice.com.

5. Uninform Law Commissions, Uniform Collaborative Law Act, www.uniformlaws.org.

6. Special thanks to the Collaborative Practice San Mateo County for permission to reprint its illustrations that so aptly capture the flow of a collaborative divorce.

7. Douglas Stone, Bruce Patton, and Sheila Heen, *Difficult Conversations: How to Discuss What Matters Most* (New York: Penguin, 2010).

PART I: THE BASIC STRUCTURE OF A DIVORCE

1. Printed with permission from Many Rivers Press; David Whyte, "To Break a Promise," in David Whyte, *Essentials*. ©ManyRivers Press, Langley, WA, 2020, www.davidwhyte.com.

CHAPTER 1. FACING REALITY IS NOT FUN, BUT IT IS NECESSARY

1. E. Mavis Hetherington and John Kelly, *For Better or for Worse: Divorce Reconsidered* (New York: Norton, 2003).
2. Elisabeth Kübler-Ross, *On Death and Dying: What the Dying Have to Teach Doctors, Nurses, Clergy and Their Own Families* (New York: Scribner, 2014).

CHAPTER 3. FIND A LAWYER YOU CAN TRUST: GOOD LAWYERS ARE WORTH THEIR WEIGHT IN GOLD

1. Bryan Stevenson, *Just Mercy: A Story of Justice and Redemption* (New York: Spiegel & Grau, 2014).

CHAPTER 4. KEEP THE FOCUS ON YOURSELF: STOP BLAMING AND PROJECTING

1. Grant Hillary Brenner, MD, FAPA, "Is Projection the Most Powerful Defense Mechanism?," *Psychology Today*, September 9, 2018, https://www.psychologytoday.com/us/blog/experimentations/201809/is-projection-the-most-powerful-defense-mechanism.
2. Pema Chödrön, "The Fundamental Ambiguity of Being Human: How to Live Beautifully with Uncertainty and Change," *Tricycle*, Fall 2012, https://tricycle.org/magazine/fundamental-ambiguity-being-human/.

CHAPTER 5. HOW TO BE YOUR BEST SELF DURING YOUR DIVORCE

1. James Hollis, PhD, *Why Good People Do Bad Things: Understanding Our Darker Selves* (New York: Gotham, 2017).
2. Carol R. Hughes and Bruce R. Fredenburg, *Home Will Never Be the Same Again: A Guide for Adult Children of Gray Divorce* (Lanham, MD: Rowman & Littlefield, 2020).
3. "Hament vs. Baker," JUSTIA US Law, https://law.justia.com/cases/vermont/supreme-court/2014/2013-220.html (accessed July 2021).
4. Hughes and Fredenberg, *Home Will Never Be the Same Again*, 2020.
5. Andrew E. Clark and Yannis Georgellis, "Back to Baseline in Britain: Adaptation in the British Household Panel Survey," *Economica* 80, no. 319 (December 2012): 496–512, https://doi.org/10.1111/ecca.12007, cited by Theresa

Boyle, "Women Happier Than Men After Divorce, Study Finds," *Toronto Star*, July 11, 2013, https://www.thestar.com/life/2013/07/11/marital_split_women _happier_after_divorce_study.html.

CHAPTER 6. LET'S GET DOWN
TO COLLABORATIVE BUSINESS

1. Road map, courtesy of Vermont Collaborative Practice.
2. Kate Scharff and Lisa Herrick, *Navigating Emotional Currents in Collaborative Divorce: A Guide to Enlightened Team Practice* (Chicago: American Bar Association, 2011).
3. Nesting is the idea that the children stay put in the marital home, and the parents make a plan for coming and going so that they can still parent the children in the comfort of home but with the freedom of not having to deal with the spouse at the same time, which can be awkward if the communication is not quite up to par.

CHAPTER 7. THE POWER OF AN
AUTHENTIC APOLOGY AT THE RIGHT TIME

1. René de Haas, Annelies Verhoeff, and J. Mark Weiss, "The Importance of the 'Scheidingsmelding'—The Good Process in Divorce," *Collaborative Review* 19, no. 1 (Spring 2020): 53.
2. Haas, Verhoeff, and Weiss, "The Importance of the 'Scheidingsmelding.'"
3. Megan Price, "Change through Curiosity in the Insight Approach to Conflict," *Revista de Mediación* 11, no. 1 (November 2017).

CHAPTER 8. ARE YOU READY TO BE DIVORCED?

1. David Whyte, "Essentials" (Langley, WA: Many Rivers Press, 2020), full poem reprinted with permission.
2. Elisabeth Kübler-Ross, *On Death and Dying: What the Dying Have to Teach Doctors, Nurses, Clergy and Their Own Families* (New York: Scribner, 2014).
3. Current preliminary research confirm the connection between divorce and grief. Z. B. Klurfeld, T. Buqo, W. C. Sanderson, and E. F. Ward-Ciesielski, "Comparing the Nature of Grief and Growth in Bereaved, Divorced, and Unemployed Individuals," *Journal of Affective Disorders* 274 (2020) 1126–1133.
4. *Diagnostic and Statistical Manual of Mental Disorders*, 5th ed. (Washington, DC: American Psychiatric Association.

CHAPTER 9. THE LEGAL LOGISTICS: WHAT TO EXPECT

1. "Highlights of Women's Earnings in 2020," U.S. Bureau of Labor Statistics, September 2021, https://www.bls.gov/opub/reports/womens-earnings/2020/home.htm.

2. Adam Kahane, *Collaborating with the Enemy: How to Work with People You Don't Agree with or Like or Trust* (Oakland, CA: Berrett-Koehler, 2017).

3. Website for Jacinta Gallant, www.Jacintagallant.ca.

CHAPTER 10. MOVE CONFIDENTLY FORWARD INTO YOUR FUTURE

1. https://ottoscharmer.com/.

2. Henna Inam's 2020 interview of Otto Scharmer, Management Sloan School of Management, "How to Co-Create with Stakeholders in Your Ecosystem," www.transformleaders.tv, episode 9. For more information about the concept of "presencing" and learning from the emergent future, see www.ottoscharmer.com.

3. Robert Keegan and Lisa Laskow Lahey, "The Real Reason People Won't Change," *Harvard Business Review*, November 2001, www.hbr.com. See also Robert Keegan and Lisa Laskow Lahey, "Immunity to Change: How to Overcome It and Unlock the Potential in Yourself and Your Organization" (Harvard Business Press, 2009).

4. Check out Susan Palmer's library of resources where she provides insightful book reviews on the latest provocative, cutting-edge leadership principles, which not only apply to systems and organizations, but I believe can be applied to the individual for expansive personal growth opportunities; www.susanpalmerconsulting.com.

5. Dalai Lama and Desmond Tutu, with Douglas Abrams, *The Book of Joy: Lasting Happiness in a Changing World* (New York: Avery, 2016).

6. Jalal Al-Din Rumi, *Rumi: Selected Poems*, trans. Coleman Barks with John Moyne, A. J. Arberry, and Reynold Nicholson (New York: HarperCollins, 1995). Reprinted with permission.

7. Esther Perel, *The State of Affairs: Rethinking Infidelity* (London: Yellow Kite, Hodder & Stoughton, 2017), 15.

Bibliography

Brenner, Grant Hillary, MD, FAPA. "Is Projection the Most Powerful Defense Mechanism?," *Psychology Today*, September 9, 2018, https://www.psy chologytoday.com/us/blog/experimentations/201809/is-projection-the-most -powerful-defense-mechanism.

Chödrön, Pema. "The Fundamental Ambiguity of Being Human: How to Live Beautifully with Uncertainty and Change," *Tricycle*, Fall 2012, https://tri cycle.org/magazine/fundamental-ambiguity-being-human.

Clark, Andrew E., and Yannis Georgellis. "Back to Baseline in Britain: Adaptation in the British Household Panel Survey," *Economica* 80, no. 319 (December 2012): 496–512, https://doi.org/10.1111/ecca.12007, cited by Theresa Boyle, "Women Happier Than Men After Divorce, Study Finds," *Toronto Star*, July 11, 2013, https://www.thestar.com/life/2013/07/11/mari tal_split_women_happier_after_divorce_study.html.

de Haas, René, Annelies Verhoeff, and Mark J. Weiss. "The Importance of the 'Scheidingsmelding'—The Good Process in Divorce," *Collaborative Review* 19, no. 1 (Spring 2020): 53.

The Diagnostic and Statistical Manual of Mental Disorders, 5th ed. Arlington, VA: American Psychiatric Association, 2013.

Hetherington, E. Mavis, and John Kelly. *For Better or for Worse: Divorce Reconsidered*. New York: Norton, 2003.

Hollis, James, PhD. *Why Good People Do Bad Things*. New York: Gotham, 2017.

Hughes, Carol R., and Bruce R. Fredenburg. *Home Will Never Be the Same Again: A Guide for Adult Children of Gray Divorce*. Lanham, MD: Rowman & Littlefield, 2020.

Inam, Henna. "How to Co-Create with Stakeholders in Your Ecosystem," www.transformleaders.tv, episode 9.

Kahane, Adam. *Collaborating with the Enemy: How to Work with People You Don't Agree with or Like or Trust*. Oakland, CA: Berrett-Koehler, 2017.

Keegan, Robert, and Lisa Laskow Lahey. "The Real Reason People Won't Change," *Harvard Business Review*, November 2001, www.hbr.com. See also Robert Keegan and Lisa Laskow Lahey, *Immunity to Change: How to Overcome It and Unlock the Potential in Yourself and Your Organization.* Harvard Business Press, 2009.

Klurfeld, Z.B., Buqo, T, W. Sanderson, C., and Ward-Ciesielski, E. F. "Comparing the Nature of Grief and Growth in Bereaved, Divorced, and Unemployed Individuals," *Journal of Affective Disorders* 274 (2020) 1126–1133.

Kübler-Ross, Elisabeth. *On Death and Dying: What the Dying Have to Teach Doctors, Nurses, Clergy and Their Own Families.* New York: Scribner, 2014.

Lama, Dalai, and Desmond Tutu, with Douglas Abrams. *The Book of Joy: Lasting Happiness in a Changing World.* New York: Avery, 2016.

Perel, Esther. *The State of Affairs: Rethinking Infidelity.* London: Yellow Kite, Hodder & Stoughton, 2017.

Price, Megan. "Change through Curiosity in the Insight Approach to Conflict," *Revista de Mediación* 11, no. 1 (November 2017).

Rumi, Jalal Al-Din. *Rumi: Selected Poems*, trans. Coleman Barks with John Moyne, A. J. Arberry, and Reynold Nicholson. New York: HarperCollins, 1995.

Scharff, Kate, and Lisa Herrick. *Navigating Emotional Currents in Collaborative Divorce: A Guide to Enlightened Team Practice.* Chicago: American Bar Association, 2011.

Stone, Douglas, Bruce Patton, and Sheila Heen. *Difficult Conversations: How to Discuss What Matters Most.* New York: Penguin, 2010.

Tesler, Pauline H., and Peggy Thompson, *Collaborative Divorce: The Revolutionary New Way to Restructure Your Family, Resolve Legal Issues, and Move on with Your Life.* New York: William Morrow, 2007.

Webb, Stuart G., and Ron Ousky. *The Collaborative Way to Divorce: The Revolutionary Method That Results in Less Stress, Lower Costs, and Happier Kids—Without Going to Court.* New York: Hudson Street Press, 2006.

Whyte, David. "Essentials." Langley, WA: Many Rivers Press, 2020.

Index

mediators, 5–6; defining, 41–42;
traditional, 45; training, 38; types
of, 40–41; use of, 38–41
men. *See* gender identity
mental health, 10; of children, 91
mental health coaches. *See* coaches
mental health neutrals, 91
mental health professionals, 3, 22–
23, 72–73; finding, 25–26
Michelangelo, 114
micromanaging, 65
mid-term marriages: affairs in, 92;
with children, 94–99; without
children, 92–94; child support
and, 94; love in, 97; marital
dynamics in, 95
mistakes, 81; emotional intelligence
and, 125–26
moral failings, divorce as, 26–27

narratives, 111; in long-term
marriages, 101–3; shared, 79–81,
93, 94
negativity, divorce lawyers and, 12
negotiation process, 116–17; in
collaborative divorce, 143–44;
direct, 33–34; emotions in, 110;
good-faith, 163; in mediation,
145
nesting, 118, 179n3
new relationships, 72–73, 155–56
no-fault divorces, 135
no-fault grounds, 36–37
nonresponsiveness, 65–66

objections, 37
off-line communication, 99
On Death and Dying (Kübler-Ross),
131
organizational development, 150
Ousky, Ron, 2–3

pain, 115
Palmer, Susan, 151, 180n4
paperwork, 6
paradigm shift, 115–16
paradoxical intervention, 122
paralegals, 59
parenting: abusive, 90; child
alignment with one parent, 142;
collaborative divorce model and,
90–91; communication and, 99;
legal logistics on agreements
about, 142–43; schedules,
110, 111; slandering in, 31;
stepparents, 98. *See also* co-
parenting
participation agreement: abuse of
collaborative divorce process,
166–67; cautions in, 164–65;
in collaborative divorce, 4;
confidentiality in, 169; draft,
105–6; enforceability of, 167;
final agreements in, 167; financial
costs in, 165; goals in, 163;
good-faith negotiation in, 163;
legal process in, 167; out of
court resolution in, 163–64; peer
review waiver, 169; rights and
obligations pending settlement,
166; roles in, 164–65; signing,
9–10; temporary agreements
in, 167; termination of, 167;
withdrawal from, 167–68
"peas in a pod" relationship, 49–52
peer review waiver, 169
Perel, Esther, 154
perfectionism, 126, 129
personal growth, 72
personality disorder, 10
personality types, 104
personal property, 93; in adversarial
divorce, 25; division of, 139–40;

About the Author

Nanci A. Smith, Esq., is an attorney licensed to practice in Vermont and New York. She is the chair of the Collaborative Divorce section of the Vermont Bar Association. She is a leader in her collaborative divorce practice group, and a member of the International Academy of Collaborative Professionals. She frequently writes and talks about divorce, family law, ethics, and collaborative divorce practices. She believes a good divorce is possible when you show up for it with humility, compassion, and the correct support.